To George Brown Tindall

CONTENTS

The Walter Lynwood Fleming
Lectures in Southern History
Louisiana State University

FROM GEORGE WALLACE TO NEWT GINGRICH

FROM
GEORGE WALLACE TO NEWT GINGRICH

RACE IN THE CONSERVATIVE COUNTERREVOLUTION, 1963–1994

DAN T. CARTER

LOUISIANA STATE UNIVERSITY PRESS
Baton Rouge

Copyright © 1996 by Louisiana State University Press
All rights reserved
Manufactured in the United States of America
Louisiana Paperback Edition, 1999
08 07 06 05 04 03 02 01 00 99
5 4 3 2 1
Designer: Amanda McDonald Key
Typeface: Times Roman
Typesetter: Impressions Book and Journal Services, Inc.

Library of Congress Cataloging-in-Publication Data:

Carter, Dan T.
    From George Wallace to Newt Gingrich : race in the conservative
counterrevolution, 1963–1994 / Dan T. Carter.
        p.   cm. — (The Walter Lynwood Fleming lectures in southern
history)
      Includes index.
        ISBN 0-8071-2118-5 (cloth); ISBN 0-8071-2366-8 (paper)
      1. United States—Race relations.   2. United States—Politics and
government—1945–1989.   3. United States—Politics and
government—1989–   4. Conservatism—United States—History—20th
century.   I. Title.   II. Series.
    E185.625.C37   1996
    305.8′00973—dc20   96-28201
                                                                         CIP

PREFACE

In early 1963, the Harris County, Texas, Republican Party elected as its chairman the youthful president and chief executive officer of Zapata Off-Shore Oil Company. George Bush, son of the wealthy and patrician Republican senator Prescott Bush Jr. of Connecticut, had made his fortune in the Texas business community; he next intended to make his mark in politics. In September of that year, he decided to run for the United States Senate seat held by Texas Democrat Ralph Yarborough.

It was an audacious move for a thirty-eight-year-old businessman who had never held elective office, but Yarborough's liberal voting record—specifically his decision to support the civil rights legislation introduced by President John Kennedy in June of 1963—made him vulnerable. Bush had staked out a position as a moderate and had welcomed blacks into the ranks of the Texas Republican Party, but on the day he announced his candidacy, he told the crowd of newsmen and supporters he would be "emphatically opposed" to the Kennedy civil rights legislation, particularly its provisions guaranteeing blacks equal access to restaurants, hotels, restrooms, and other public accommodations. What counted was a "person's heart in the civil rights quest," he said. Legal coercion was counterproductive.[1]

As the 1964 campaign accelerated, Bush watched the progress of Alabama's George Wallace. In March of that year, Wallace had entered the Wisconsin Democratic presidential primary in what seemed a bizarre venture for a Deep South governor already typecast by the media as a race-baiting Dixie demagogue. Although he insisted that his was a campaign to maintain constitutional principles, no one who knew Wallace's history

1. Dallas *Morning News,* September 12, 1963; San Antonio *Express,* September 12, 1963; Houston *Chronicle,* September 12, 1963.

or listened to his slashing attacks on the Kennedy/Johnson civil rights proposals ever doubted the centrality of race in his appeal to voters.

Wisconsin's Catholic hierarchy and the entire Protestant religious establishment, the state's Democratic Party, and organized labor condemned Wallace as a bigot and an "apostle of discord." Three weeks before the election, Wisconsin's governor predicted the southerner would not receive 10 percent of the primary vote. On election day, however, 34 percent of the voters chose Wallace. Three weeks later in Indiana, with two Ku Klux Klansmen coordinating the Wallace campaign out of the phone booth of a filling station, the Alabamian took 30 percent of the primary vote. In Maryland he claimed 43 percent and—as he always darkly suggested afterward—"that was with them countin' the votes."[2]

Wallace's astonishing achievement decisively confirmed George Bush's conviction that most Americans—certainly most white Texans—would not support a candidate who backed the Civil Rights Act. On the day after Wallace's surprise finish in Wisconsin, Bush told a reporter for the Dallas *Morning News* that the Alabama governor's success at appealing to northern voters showed that there was a "general concern from many responsible people over the civil rights bill all over the nation."[3]

In June, after Lyndon Johnson pushed through the Civil Rights Act of 1964, George Wallace bowed out of the presidential race, deferring to conservative Republican Barry Goldwater, who had broken ranks with most of his GOP colleagues by voting against the federal civil rights bill. Meanwhile, George Bush had vanquished his Republican primary opponents. Packing away his Ivy League button-down shirts, he chartered a

2. Wallace's press secretary, Bill Jones, describes the inside of the 1964 campaigns with a fair degree of candor in *The Wallace Story* (Northport, Ala.: American Southern Publishing Co., 1966), 104–346. See also Jody Carlson, *George C. Wallace and the Politics of Powerlessness: The Wallace Campaigns for the Presidency, 1964–1976* (New Brunswick, N.J.: Transaction Books, 1981), 27–66; M. Margaret Conway, "The White Backlash Reexamined: Wallace and the 1964 Primaries," *Social Science Quarterly,* XLIX (1968), 710–19; Richard C. Haney, "Wallace in Wisconsin: The Presidential Primary of 1964," *Wisconsin Magazine of History,* LXI (1978), 255–70; Matthew E. Welsh, "Civil Rights and the Primary Election of 1964 in Indiana: The Wallace Challenge," *Indiana Magazine of History,* LXXV (1979), 1–27; and John Joseph Makay, "The Speaking of Governor George C. Wallace in the 1964 Maryland Primary" (Ph.D. dissertation, Purdue University, 1969).

3. Dallas *Morning News,* April 9, 11, 1964.

bus and hit the road with his own country-western band. The Black Mountain Boys began each rally with the spirited refrain: "The sun's going to shine in the Senate some day / George Bush is going to chase them liberals away." In his standard stump speech, Bush labeled the Civil Rights Act—backed by the "ultra-liberal Ralph Yarborough"—an abuse of federal power, one that "trampled upon the Constitution." Speaking to a north Texas rally in September, Bush ripped a page straight out of George Wallace's speeches when he warned salaried workers they would be "displaced" by the antidiscrimination provisions of the bill. "The new civil rights act was passed to protect 14 percent of the people," he explained to a crowd of four hundred white employees at the Ling-Temco-Vought Corporation in Grand Prairie, Texas. "I'm also worried about the other 86 percent."[4]

In November, Barry Goldwater, who had temporarily replaced George Wallace as the Great White Hope for those Americans most hostile to civil rights, went down to a smashing defeat by Lyndon Johnson. Texas Democrat Ralph Yarborough brushed aside his Republican challenger, George Bush, and returned to the Senate by a twelve-point margin.

But Goldwater, Johnson, and Yarborough were moving from center stage. Wallace and Bush would continue to command major roles in American politics. During the period historians have called "the Second Reconstruction," these two men and their contemporaries would grapple with what Gunnar Myrdal so rightly termed "an American Dilemma": the politics of race.

In the spring of 1991, as I continued my research on a biography of Alabama's governor George Wallace, I delivered the Walter Lynwood Fleming Lectures at Louisiana State University. Over the course of nearly five years of research, I had become convinced that the shadow of this fiery politician reached far beyond his own national career from 1964 to 1976.

Historians of the American left have made much of the way in which the civil rights movement influenced social movements of the 1960s and

4. Jefferson Morley, "Bush and the Blacks: An Unknown Story," *New York Review of Books,* January 16, 1992, p. 21; Austin *American,* September 25, 1964; Dallas *Morning News,* October 28, 1964.

1970s, inspiring, for example, the women's rights movement and the politics of sexual liberation. But the movement's counterrevolutionary effects are equally important. In the three decades following the emergence of George Wallace, the rhetoric of racial politics evolved: from the issues of public accommodations to school desegregation, busing, housing, quotas and struggles over job discrimination, and proposals for economic affirmative action.

What is less clear is the path by which the politics of racial conservatism broadened into a general program of resistance to the changes sweeping American society. Economic and social conservatives—particularly those who have been lifelong opponents of racial bigotry—have bridled at the attempt to link what neoconservatives have called the "new majoritarianism" of the 1980s with the politics of race. Nevertheless, I think it is fair to say that even though the streams of racial and economic conservatism have sometimes flowed in separate channels, they ultimately joined in the political coalition that reshaped American politics from the 1970s through the mid-1990s.

Republicans benefiting from this shift in their political fortunes have extravagantly praised Ronald Reagan as patron saint and acknowledged their debts to Barry Goldwater and Richard Nixon. They have even suborned Franklin Roosevelt to the cause of Republican conservatism. But George Wallace remains a figure to be ignored in the fervent hope that he will quietly disappear out the back door of our historical memory.

The reluctance of neoconservatives to claim Wallace—with his gamy aura of racism—is understandable. But the fundamental differences between the public rhetoric of the Alabama governor and the new conservativism sometimes seem more a matter of style than substance. In Barry Goldwater's vote against the Civil Rights Bill of 1964, in Richard Nixon's subtle manipulation of the busing issue, in Ronald Reagan's genial demolition of affirmative action, in George Bush's use of the Willie Horton ads, and in Newt Gingrich's demonization of welfare mothers, the Wallace music played on. The new rhetoric—carefully tested and marketed by political consultants—may lack Wallace's visceral edge (and wit), but it reflects the same callous political exploitation of the raw wounds of racial division in our country.

Of course, race as an issue in American politics has consistently evolved since George Wallace took his message north in the winter of 1963. In the Fleming Lectures, I sought to explore that evolution as reflected in the presidential politics of the last three decades, a period during which we have experienced economic upheaval and the structural transformation of the very fabric of American politics. The American Dilemma has existed since the foundations of the Republic, but Wallace and the six presidents who followed Lyndon Johnson have all had to confront that dilemma in the context of a communications revolution, the breakdown of the traditional party system, and the public's increasingly cynical attitude toward the political process.

In bringing the story into the mid-1990s, I have added a fourth chapter to the original three lectures. For a historian, to reflect is to revise, and I have been sorely tempted to modify my original remarks. Today, for example, I would be more inclined to emphasize the ways in which racially charged political advertising was a reflection rather than a causative factor in the decline of those inhibitions that had characterized Americans' discussion of racial issues. And I suspect I would be more critical of the failure of Democratic politicians to confront creatively the growing erosion of national support for civil rights.

But I have decided to leave the text of the lectures essentially unchanged. If, as a historian, I am foolhardy enough to write about what are essentially current events, I should be willing to acknowledge the misjudgments of my earlier assessments.

The department of history of Louisiana State University asked me to deliver the Fleming Lectures and extended their usual warm hospitality during my visit. During my 1995–1996 appointment as Pitt Professor at Cambridge University and a fellow of Sidney Sussex College, fellow historians at the Universities of Cambridge, Oxford, Keele, Sheffield, Genoa, and Odense and at University College, London, listened to my ruminations on the issue of race and recent American politics and responded with generous and insightful criticism. I am grateful as well for the financial support of my own institution, Emory University, and the National Humanities Center, which awarded me an NEH fellowship for 1990–1991.

FROM GEORGE WALLACE TO NEWT GINGRICH

1 | THE POLITICS OF ANGER

In 1963, George Wallace moved from the stage of regional politics into the national consciousness. Only a small number of Americans had heard him before his inauguration as governor of Alabama in January of 1963, when the ferocity of his defense of the white South captured their attention. Then and now, most Americans remember little about his inaugural address beyond the famous line, "Segregation now! Segregation tomorrow! Segregation forever!"[1] That amnesia has allowed Wallace to insist that his defense of segregation was a symbolic issue; his struggle was to preserve states' rights against the overweening power of the federal government. As he said on several occasions in attempting to dismiss the significance of that speech, he should have said "States' rights now! States' rights tomorrow! States' rights forever!" He was never against black people; his oratory had nothing to do with race.[2]

Nothing could be further from the truth.

By the Deep South standards of the 1950s, the Alabamian had been a

1. All three major networks used the "segregation forever" section of his speech in their evening broadcasts. The Associated Press, United Press International, the New York *Times,* and both major afternoon papers in Alabama opened with it.

2. James Wooten, "George Wallace: The Island of his Exile," *Washington Post Magazine,* April 1, 1984, p. 13. As Wallace told Howell Raines in 1979 in commenting on his inaugural address, "I made a mistake in the sense that I should have clarified my position more. I was never saying anything that reflected upon black people, and I'm very sorry that it was taken that way." New York *Times,* January 21, 1979.

liberal on economic issues and a moderate on race, but his bitter loss to John Patterson in June of 1958 marked a turning point. After early returns made it clear that he would lose decisively, a depressed Wallace waited with several close friends in a car parked outside the Jefferson Davis Hotel, postponing the dreaded concession speech he would have to make to his followers. "Well, boys," he said tightly as he snuffed out his cigar, "no other son-of-a-bitch will ever out-nigger me again." [3]

The man who wrote George Wallace's inaugural address was Asa Carter, founder and coeditor of the *Southerner,* one of the most racist magazines published in the 1950s. Although Carter publicly described himself as a White Citizens Council leader, he was in reality a professional anti-Semite and hard-line racial terrorist, the organizer of a secret paramilitary force with the romantic name "Original Ku Klux Klan of the Confederacy." His speech at Clinton, Tennessee, in March of 1957 kicked off a race riot, and on one occasion he shot and seriously wounded two Klan followers who challenged his leadership. Carter's Klan group helped organize the riots at the University of Alabama that led to Autherine Lucy's expulsion in February of 1956. The following month, six of his men carried out an assault on the black singer Nat "King" Cole as he performed before an all-white audience in Birmingham, and four hard-core members of the Klavern seized, at random, a Birmingham black handyman as he walked along a country road and castrated him as a warning to civil rights activists.

This was the man Wallace chose as his main speechwriter for the 1962

3. Marshall Frady used the "out-niggered" (or "out-nigguhed") quotation in his 1968 biography of the Alabama governor, but Wallace later denied making the statement, and his official biographer, Stephen Lesher, has defended that claim. Although Bill Jones, Wallace's press aide, who was there that night, now says that "my memory fails me about the 'I won't be out-niggered again,'" Starr Smith, who was also present, emphatically recalls the exchange. Moreover, Wallace made the same statement to Seymore Trammell the day after the election, and he was still repeating it four years later. Starr Smith to author, June 1, 1994; Marshall Frady, *Wallace* (2d ed.; New York: New American Library, 1976), 127; Stephen Lesher, *George Wallace: American Populist* (Reading, Mass.: Addison-Wesley Publishing Co., 1994), 129; Starr Smith to author, June 1, 1994; Bill Jones to author, July 11, 1994; Author's interview with Seymore Trammell, November 28, 1989; "Report from Benjamin Muse," February 6, 1964, Benjamin Muse Reports, Southern Regional Council Papers, Woodruff Library, Atlanta University.

governor's race; this was the man he chose to write the defining speech of his life. Wallace's inaugural was, in fact, little more than an amalgam of Carter's apocalyptic monthly articles from his hate magazine. The defense of segregation did not symbolize the larger issues of states' rights; racial purity lay at the very core of southern defiance. A "basically ungodly government," led by the United States Supreme Court, warned Wallace, sought to "play at being God . . . without faith in God . . . and without the wisdom of God." That governmental apparatus fed and encouraged "everything degenerate and base in our people" with its substitution of "what it calls 'human rights' for individual rights."

Communism was winning the world, Wallace told a cheering audience of 12,000. America was being betrayed by the liberals who followed the "false doctrine of communistic amalgamation." And "if we amalgamate into the one unit as advocated by these communist philosophers . . . then the enrichment of our lives . . . the freedom for our development . . . is gone forever. We become, therefore, a mongrel unit of one under a single, all powerful government."[4]

The reckless course embarked on by the nation's leaders was worse than that of the Nazis. The "*national* racism of Hitler's Germany persecuted a *national* minority to the whim of a *national* majority," noted Wallace, but the "*international* racism of the liberals seek to persecute the *international* white minority to the whim of the *international* colored majority."

To make certain that no one had any doubts about what he meant, Wallace pointed to the recent black violence that had claimed the lives of whites living in the former Belgian Congo. "Those Belgian survivors of the Congo," Wallace reminded his listeners, could not present their case to a "war crimes commission." And neither, he added, could the citizens of Oxford, Mississippi.[5]

During the next decade, political observers would concoct fanciful

4. "Original Inaugural Address of the Honorable George C. Wallace, Governor of Alabama, January 14, 1963," in Alabama Department of Archives and History, Montgomery, Alabama (hereinafter cited as ADAH).

5. It is doubtful if Wallace realized the implication of his subtly invidious comparison between racial liberals and Nazis, but Carter—a devoted anti-Semite and secret defender of Hitler—certainly did.

scenarios in which a minority of voters elected the Alabama governor as president; even Wallace, in his unguarded moments, would seriously entertain the belief that he might someday be the nation's chief executive.

It was fantasy. If most Americans, indeed most Alabamians, remembered few of the details of his oration, the racial implications of his segregation pledge were clear enough. Wallace's 1963 inaugural speech was his Faustian bargain. It guaranteed his national notoriety; it also doomed him to work along the boundaries of American politics. But what a periphery it was! In the months after his inauguration, Wallace demonstrated his political skills as he brilliantly repositioned himself away from the narrowly racial rhetoric of his 1962 gubernatorial campaign and adopted a kind of soft-porn racism in which fear and hatred could be mobilized without mentioning race itself (except to deny that he was a racist). The key turning point—his Stand in the Schoolhouse Door—lets us see something of the critical interaction between the issues of race and politics and the increasingly powerful role played by television.

In June of 1963, George Wallace fulfilled his pledge to block the entrance of two black students to the University of Alabama. More than two hundred newspaper reporters converged on the Tuscaloosa campus for this highly staged event. Our collective memory is shaped not by words, however, but by the grainy black-and-white images of that day's television news cameras. United States Assistant Attorney General Nicholas Katzenbach strides up the long walkway to the entrance of Carmichael Hall; Wallace stands in the blistering summer heat and sternly raises one hand like an irascible traffic cop; the governor attacks the "illegal usurpation of power by the Central Government" and insists that he will stand firm to "forbid this illegal and unwarranted action by the Central Government."

It was, of course, a theatrical performance, staged for the benefit of a national television audience. Within two hours the federal government had nationalized the Alabama National Guard, Wallace had backed down, the students had been enrolled, and the governor had returned to Montgomery. Leaders of both parties, the media, and other national-opinion shapers all agreed the Stand in the Schoolhouse Door was simply one more shabby charade in a long line of presentations by southern demagogues.

Wallace, predicted one usually astute reporter, would soon be "placed beside that old broken musketeer, Ross Barnett, in Dixie's wax museum."[6]

They were wrong. George Wallace instinctively understood the lesson that media specialists would slowly grasp: in the world of television, viewers' opinions were shaped by the powerful totality of visual and verbal "impressions," impressions that could be molded and directed in such a way as to overwhelm earlier notions and ideas, particularly those not firmly fixed in the viewer's mind.

First, the television coverage gave Wallace stature. According to an old Arab proverb, "A man with powerful enemies is a powerful man." By claiming center stage with the representative of the president of the United States—a representative who had to treat him with respect and even deference—Wallace transformed himself into a major player in American politics.

Second, by producing a relatively dignified media event, the Alabama governor showed that he understood the old adage that a picture (or, in this case, a series of pictures) is worth a thousand words. The print media might describe the complexities of Wallace's involvement in racist politics, but what 78 million viewers saw on the three major networks' evening news programs were clips that ranged in length from four minutes twenty seconds to six minutes thirty-five seconds. George Wallace appeared indignant but poised, his language a little stilted and pretentious but nothing like the raving demagoguery most Americans expected to hear.

Attorney General Robert Kennedy had chosen to position Vivian Malone and Jimmy Hood offstage, in a government sedan at the curb, to shield them from a direct confrontation with the governor. It was a long-range blunder for the Kennedy administration. *If* the two had stood beside Katzenbach, viewers, rather than seeing George Wallace make a declaration of "constitutional principles," would have seen him holding up his hand, physically blocking two qualified black applicants. In the short run, the presence of Malone and Hood would have helped Wallace. In the long

---

6. Statement and Proclamation of Governor George C. Wallace, University of Alabama, June 11, 1963, File Drawer 443, "University of Alabama: Segregation" File, Alabama Governors' Papers, ADAH; Robert G. Sherrill, "Wallace and the Future of Dixie," *Nation,* CXCIX (October 26, 1964), 266.

run, their presence would have made it difficult to insist that race was irrelevant.

But the performance succeeded. Few nonsoutherners wanted to embrace overt racism in 1963. Wallace's use of nonracial language allowed a substantial minority of Americans to maintain the illusion that the issue was indeed an abstract constitutional question. In the week following his television performance, more than 100,000 congratulatory telegrams and letters flooded the office of the Alabama governor. Over half came from outside the South, and 95 percent supported George Wallace.[7]

As NBC's Douglas Kiker said, it was a moment of epiphany for George Wallace. He had looked out upon those white Americans north of Alabama and suddenly been awakened by a blinding vision: "They all hate black people, all of them. They're all afraid, all of them. Great God! That's it! They're all Southern! The whole United States is Southern!"[8] Most Americans, of course, continued to regard him with disdain, but the response to his Tuscaloosa performance confirmed the governor's belief that a large floating constituency awaited a champion. Six months earlier, he had discussed the possibility of a presidential campaign to mobilize opposition to racial integration, but it is not clear that he intended his candidacy as more than a symbolic gesture.[9] In the aftermath to the Stand in the Schoolhouse Door, George Wallace began to gear up for a national campaign.

There is today a great debate about the space that should be allowed between a candidate's public and private positions. No one who knew

7. Author's interview with Bill Jones, August 3, 1990.

8. Douglas Kiker, "Red Neck New York: Is This Wallace Country?" *New York,* October 7, 1968, p. 25.

9. In the twenty-four hours preceding his inauguration in 1963, Wallace quietly met with a group of segregationist southern political leaders to hear a proposal from a right-wing Virginia newspaperman, John Synon. Synon had been inspired by the 1960 presidential election—an election so close that the electoral votes of Mississippi, Alabama, South Carolina, Louisiana, Arkansas, and Georgia could have held the balance of power. Synon's original plan was to push a group of favorite sons from each Deep South state—for example, Barnett in Mississippi, Wallace in Alabama, Strom Thurmond in South Carolina, Harry Byrd in Virginia. Wallace was interested but uncertain that the Synon plan would promote his ambitions. Bill Jones, *The Wallace Story* (Northport, Ala.: American Southern Publishing Co., 1966), 329–32.

Wallace well ever took seriously his earnest professions—uttered a thousand times after 1963—that he was not a racist, or, as he put it in a line that reporters ultimately lip-synced to amuse themselves: "I have never made a speech or statement in my life that reflected on any man because of his race, color, creed or national origin." It is difficult to know how Americans would have reacted had they been able to glimpse the private Wallace. He was—like many southern white politicians of his class and generation—simply incapable of avoiding racial epithets. Tony Heffernan, a UPI reporter in the 1960s (and a native New Yorker), covered Wallace at close range throughout the 1960s. He "never said anything but 'Negro' in public," recalled Heffernan, "but in personal conversation, they were 'niggers.'" The staple of humorous conversation was the "nigger joke." A decade later, New York *Times* reporter Jim Wooten—no virgin on the subject of racism—was as much stunned as appalled when Wallace casually referred to Edward W. Brooke as that "nigger senator from Massachusetts." [10]

Very occasionally an interpretive piece in a major newspaper or magazine would repeat one of the Alabama governor's imprudent remarks ("All these countries with niggers in 'em have stayed the same for a thousand years"). But most of Wallace's—and other politicians'—racist slurs went unreported. The rules among newsmen in the 1960s were for the most part crudely simple, recalled one freelance writer: "You didn't report who was fucking whom, and you didn't print [those kinds of] indiscreet comments of politicians." Occasionally, although carefully avoiding the "n" word, local reporters managed to convey some sense of the ugly contours of Wallace's racial outlook. "I read where a Uganda [*sic*] leader said he didn't like the Birmingham racial situation," Ramona Martin of the Montgomery *Journal* quoted the Alabamian as telling a Mississippi audience in 1963. "I guess he [Kenya's president, Jomo Kenyatta] was leaning on his spear when he said it." That anyone might find such an observation offensive bewildered him. [11]

---

10. Howell Raines, ed., *My Soul Is Rested: The Story of the Civil Rights Movement in the Deep South* (New York: G. P. Putnam's Sons, 1977), 373–76; New York *Times*, May 7, 1972.

11. "Wallace: 'Welcome Home You Living Doll,'" *Newsweek*, June 1, 1964, p. 18; Author's interview with William Bradford Huie, March 24, 1985; Montgomery *Journal*, June 18, 1963.

Wallace seemed genuinely to believe that blacks were a separate race, inferior and threatening. In an unguarded moment early in his national political career, he confided to a Canadian social-studies teacher that the only hope for the nation was complete segregation. Not only were blacks criminally predisposed, he wrote, they were also prone to commit the most "atrocious acts of humanity, such as rape, assault and murder." Such antisocial behavior was a reflection of the fact that a "vast percentage of people who are infected with venereal diseases are people of the Negro race." In addition to their criminality and sexual promiscuity, blacks were lazy and shiftless. If black and white mingled in the schools, inevitably "this mixing will result in the races mixing socially which fact will bring about intermarriages of the races, and eventually our [white] race will be deteriated [*sic*] to that of the mongrel complexity." [12]

The depth of Wallace's racism—the degree to which it was part of his core beliefs—was always unclear. He sometimes manifested an air of apologetic cynicism; when forced to break away from informal gatherings because of a speaking engagement, he would often turn to his friends and ask to be excused with a sheepish grin and a half-embarrassed explanation: "I got to go give 'em a little nigger-talk."

Seymore Wolfbein, a Labor Department expert in the Kennedy administration, was convinced it was all an act. At the United States Governors' Conference in Miami Beach in 1963, he tuned in to a local television news program just in time to see George Wallace tearing into the Labor Department in general and Wolfbein in particular for requiring nondiscrimination in federally funded job-training programs. (The station had to bleep out a reference to Wolfbein as a "bastard.") Two hours later, Wallace grabbed Wolfbein in a hotel corridor, pulled him aside, and put his arm around him with a gesture of familiarity and friendship. The governor explained that he had "nothing against bureaucrats, white people, Jews and all the other things that I was," recalled Wolfbein. Nor was he concerned if the Labor Department developed integrated job-training programs, as long as federal officials stayed out of the newspapers and "didn't

12. Art Wallace to George Wallace, August 13, 1963, George Wallace to Art Wallace, September 13, 1963, both in Box 399, "Segregation" File, Alabama Governors' Papers, ADAH.

make too much noise about it." [13] Wolfbein found Wallace fascinating and amusing, but hardly sinister, a kind of roguish political con man eager to let him in on the joke.

When confronted with the question of whether Wallace was "sincere" in his racial views, a Montgomery attorney who knew the governor well said it best. "If George had parachuted into the Albanian countryside in the spring of 1962," reflected John Kohn, one of Wallace's advisers in the 1960s, "he would have been head of a collective farm by harvesttime, a member of the Communist Party by midwinter, on his way to the district party meeting as a delegate by the following year, and a member of the Comintern in two or three years." George, said Kohn, "could believe whatever he needed to believe." [14]

That such a southern politician should gain a national hearing suggests the extent to which "white backlash" had begun to stretch beyond the southern states. As school-desegregation decisions, antidiscrimination housing ordinances, and race riots moved north in the mid-1960s, Americans soon discovered there was a bit of redneck in Grand Rapids as well as in Birmingham. When Lyndon Johnson took office in 1963, only 31 percent of the nation's adults felt that the federal government was pushing integration "too fast." By 1968, that figure had grown to more than 50 percent. The Kennedy/Johnson civil rights measures, however limited in their impact, had reached beyond the South and confronted the existence of racial discrimination in the North in housing and employment.[15]

What is perhaps less understandable is how George Wallace tapped into those fears and escaped Dixie's history, which had trapped in regional amber such fellow demagogues as Orval Faubus, Ross Barnett, and Lester ("Axe Handle") Maddox. Wallace's enemies—and they were legion—attributed his success in transcending his regional roots to a combination of

13. Interview with Seymore Wolfbein, November 21, 1966, by Larry J. Hackman, John F. Kennedy Library Transcript.
14. Author's conversation with John Kohn, January 12, 1988.
15. The social-science research and the journalistic accounts of white backlash are voluminous. Pollster Louis Harris and William Brink summarize the growth of nonsouthern white hostility to black advances in *Black and White: A Study of U.S. Racial Attitudes Today* (New York: Simon & Schuster, 1964), 100–17. See also George H. Gallup, *The Gallup Poll: 1935–1971* (3 vols.; New York: Random House, 1972), III, 1933, 1941–43, 2011, 2021, 2128.

two factors: first, the existence of racism outside the South, and second, the support of ultraright activists and financial contributors who equated Wallace's attacks on the federal government with their hostility to "liberal" economic legislation.

It is certainly true that a sizable number of right-wing, nouveau-riche politicos supported the Alabama governor out of a hard-nosed assessment of the financial benefits his candidacy offered. Many members of the ultraright were equally attracted to Wallace's semihysterical anti-Communism. As a former assistant remembered, any trip out to meet the Wallace faithful was a tour of the radical-right bestiary: John Birchers (whose administrative skills rescued the Alabamian's 1968 presidential campaign from absolute chaos), the Minutemen, the Ku Klux Klan, the White Action Movement, and a dozen other fringe hate groups who emerged and then disappeared into the cauldron of the politics of the 1950s and 1960s.[16]

For most liberals of the 1960s and 1970s, it was an article of faith that Wallace was funded by such right-wing patrons as Texas millionaire H. L. Hunt and segregationist Louisiana oilman Leander Perez, but they were mistaken. Hunt's eccentric son, Bunker, once handed over a briefcase filled with hundred-dollar bills (variously said to total $300,000 or $400,000). But no individual or group ever controlled Wallace. He used and manipulated *them,* but the course he charted was never dictated by anyone but George Wallace. In fact, most of his money came from two sources. First, there was the venerable Alabama tradition of shaking down highway contractors, textbook suppliers, and other purveyors of state goods and services. Although this source became significant in times of financial crisis for the Wallace campaign, the governor's closest associates skimmed off

16. Author's interview with Seymore Trammell, January 11, 1988. Jack Nelson of the Los Angeles *Times* repeatedly called attention to the critical role John Birchers and other doctrinaire right-wing groups played in the Wallace campaigns of 1968 and 1972. See, for example, Los Angeles *Times,* March 18, 1968, April 11, 1972. Surprisingly, Wallace used little anti-Communist rhetoric in the 1968 campaign (in contrast to the 1964 and 1972 campaigns). Political sociologist Jody Carlson suggests that Wallace's muting of the issue in 1968 stemmed from his desire to avoid drawing attention to the strong support he received from "extremist" anti-communist organizations such as the John Birch Society. Jody Carlson, *George Wallace and the Politics of Powerlessness: The Wallace Campaigns for the Presidency, 1964–1976* (New Brunswick, N.J.: Transaction Books, 1981), 132.

much of the money. The real foundation of his campaign kitty was the hundreds of thousands of low- and middle-income Americans who mailed ten- and twenty-dollar contributions—usually in cash—to the permanent "Wallace Campaign" headquarters outside Montgomery. What seemed unbelievable to hard-boiled reporters at the time now seems entirely possible in light of the fund-raising success of today's televangelists.

Wallace, with his unadorned lust for public office, was his own secret weapon. In the 1950s, '60s, and '70s, every courthouse *philosophe* in Alabama had stories to tell of his relentless pursuit of votes and public adulation. Blessed with that memory for names and faces essential to any southern politician, Wallace could walk into a crowded room and identify every individual, some of whom he had met only briefly eight or ten years earlier. If his first biographer, Marshall Frady, was sometimes imaginative in his poetic descriptions and a little creative in his dialogue, he accurately sketched the broad contours of his subject's skills and his politics—even when he did not always understand their roots.

George Wallace came from a prosperous south Alabama family. His grandfather, a country doctor and large landowner, had been one of the most respected men in Barbour County, but by the time Wallace was born, his father had begun a slide toward poverty that would haunt young George for the rest of his life. Hard-drinking and often in poor health, the senior Wallace deeded little to his son except a pugnacious temperament and a touchy sensitivity to slights and condescension. George's mother kept the family together but was cold and distant; what meager affection she offered was reserved for her third child, the sickly Gerald.

In a classic case of compensation, Wallace early learned to ingratiate himself with everyone he met. He could, one neighbor later recalled, "charm a bird out of a tree," a talent he used with all his elders and then upon the pretty young women of small-town Clio.[17] His childhood and his experiences in college, law school, and the army forged an identity upon the twin anvils of resentment and an almost pathetic search for

17. Frady, *Wallace,* 63–73; George C. Wallace, *Stand Up for America* (Garden City, N.Y.: Doubleday & Co., 1976), 12–18; George Wallace Jr., *The Wallaces of Alabama* (Chicago: Follett Publishing Co., 1975), 18–28; Montgomery *Advertiser,* June 17, 18, 19, 1962; Author's interview with Cornelia Wallace, October 14, 1988.

affection and respect. Popular and one of the brightest members of his class at the University of Alabama, he was always aware of his "country" background and his lack of polish and sophistication. Admission into the "right" circles, where the sons of Alabama planters and businessmen formed social associations that would shape the rest of their lives, eluded him, and he privately resented what he saw as condescension and patronization by the "swells" of Montgomery and Birmingham society.[18] In the army he made friends with GIs from all over the country. He had never been particularly conscious of his southernness, but the ribbing of northern soldiers about his accent and provincialism often rankled, and helped to shape the way in which he looked at the world.

Wallace's sensitivity to being "looked down on" and his identity as a beleaguered white southerner strengthened his appeal to white ethnic minorities and working-class Americans. Many of his followers were, in the parlance of the social scientists, "alienated." Like the Populists of the late nineteenth century, Wallace supporters—North and South—felt psychologically and culturally isolated from the dominant currents of American life in the 1960s. In contrast to the Populists, neither Wallace nor his followers had any understanding of, or deep interest in, the workings of the American economic system. But like the Populists, they were deeply embittered over the way in which respectable folk sniggered at their lack of cultural sophistication. No Wallace speech was complete without the defensive claim that he and his supporters were "just as cultured and refined" as those "New York reporters."[19]

The peculiar complexity of "provincial" Alabama politics both strengthened and limited Wallace's national role. We tend to forget that he began his career as a protégé of one of the most liberal southern politicians in modern history, James ("Big Jim"—"Kissing Jim") Folsom. As

18. Frady, *Wallace,* 74–82; Joe Terry interview with Bill Jones, March 7, 1986, as part of the Wallace Project of University of Alabama Public Television (hereinafter cited as APT Interviews). The Jones interview is one of more than fifty conducted by producer Joe Terry and associate producer Camille Elebash for a two-hour documentary on the Alabama governor. The interviews are not transcribed; I have viewed the 108 hours of videotapes and transcribed what I consider to be the most important portions.

19. Ray Jenkins, APT Interview. This defensiveness is a theme of "Wallace-watcher" Brandt Ayers, former editor of the Anniston (Ala.) *Star.* Brandt Ayers, APT Interview.

a delegate to the 1948 national Democratic convention, Wallace stayed with the party loyalists and refused to join the racist Dixiecrat walkout for Strom Thurmond. In the state legislature, he consistently introduced legislation to aid disadvantaged Alabamians. Even on racial issues he was a moderate, conscientiously serving as a member of the board of trustees of the all-black Tuskegee Institute (though he later tried to make light of his apostasy with crude jokes among fellow politicians about "spending weekends with those 'high-yaller' majorettes").[20]

Alabama, whatever its racist crudities, was not Mississippi. For more than one hundred years, yeoman farmers from the northern counties had waged a political guerrilla war against the reactionary Black Belt gentry, and the state had by southern standards a substantial organized labor movement and a vigorous tradition of working-class political activism. Few other southern states had furnished liberal politicians to match Folsom, Hugo Black, Lister Hill, and John Sparkman. Wallace's past support for New Deal liberalism (or "progressivism," as he preferred to call it) gave him an ear for the complex variant of populist conservatism that characterized blue-collar workers and disenchanted Democrats all over the nation.

His appeal to ethnic voters in the urban Northeast and Midwest initially confounded political observers. In retrospect, it is not that surprising that he drew support from these groups. The often blue-collar ethnic neighborhoods of Boston, New York, Philadelphia, Cleveland, Gary, and Chicago had borne the brunt of social transformation as the black community spread into these once-stable sections. Many, though certainly not all, such ethnic voters saw in Wallace a kindred spirit: a man despised and dismissed by distant social planners all too ready to sacrifice working-class families on the altar of upper-middle-class convictions.

All of these factors help to explain his appeal, but there is something more. The files of Governor Wallace's chief of staff, General Taylor Hardin, describe how, as early as 1966 and 1967, several Wallace staffers drew upon the computer expertise of Oklahoma preacher Billy James Hargis' Christian Anti-Communist Crusade to develop their own direct-mail fund-raising program. The portly Tulsa evangelist has long since been

---

20. Author's interview with Seymore Trammell, November 28, 1988.

overshadowed by Oral Roberts, the Bakkers, Jimmy Swaggart, and Pat Robertson, but in the mid-1960s he had 212 radio outlets and twelve television stations and was well on his way to becoming the first of the big-time Christian broadcasters—until a disgruntled associate disclosed his somewhat unfatherly interest in younger students. His fall from grace should not obscure the fact that Hargis was one of the first to grasp the way in which weekly doses of apocalyptic warnings, accompanied by computer-generated "personalized" mailings, could help charismatic demagogues tap the pocketbooks of frightened television viewers.

The red baiting that dominated every aspect of Wallace's anti-civil-rights rhetoric during these years served him well. It allowed him to use Cold War fears of international Communism to discredit the civil rights movement. And the cadences of anti-Communism gave him a rhetorical bridge to a national audience. In the early 1960s, most nonsoutherners were still ambiguous in their attitudes toward the rising civil rights movement; they were not ambiguous in their hatred for the Red Menace.

Anti-Communist rhetoric also allowed Wallace to link his crusade against black Americans to a long historical tradition of paranoia in which Americans viewed politics not as a conflict between different visions of the common good, but as a moral tableau, a religious struggle of conspiracy and betrayal in which the forces of light must constantly struggle against those of the darkness.

And Wallace was, of course, the ultimate beneficiary of a series of wrenching events in the 1960s: the race riots of the long hot summers, which spread pillars of fire across America's urban landscape; the explosion of the antiwar movement as the conflict in Vietnam accelerated after 1965; and the general sense of a collapse in traditional values in the nation's homes and streets. Liberal academics and journalists might speak evenhandedly—even approvingly—of the emergence of a counterculture. But as George Wallace looked out upon the disordered political landscape of the 1960s, he sensed that millions of Americans felt betrayed and victimized by the sinister forces of change. He knew that a substantial percentage of the American electorate despised the civil rights agitators and antiwar demonstrators as symptoms of a fundamental decline in the traditional cultural compass of God, family, and country, a decline reflected in rising crime rates, the legalization of abortion, the rise in out-of-wedlock pregnancies, the increase in divorce rates, and the proliferation of "obscene" literature and films. And moving always beneath the surface was the fear that blacks were moving beyond their safely encapsulated ghettos into "our" streets, "our" schools, "our" neighborhoods.

The Wallace campaign had begun long before 1968. His 1964 foray in the Democratic primaries of Wisconsin, Indiana, and Maryland had convinced him that his basic strategy was sound; by the spring of 1965, he and several members of his staff were talking guardedly about a third-party run. The leadership of both parties was the same, Wallace complained in the summer of 1966 as he traveled throughout the country: "You could put them all in an Alabama cotton picker's sack, shake them up and dump them out; take the first one to slide out and put him right back into power and there would be no change."[21] The ultraliberalism of the two major parties might make it necessary for him to sacrifice himself on the altar of national politics as a third-party candidate, he hinted in one speech late in 1966.

Wallace handily survived one political scare on his home grounds after a handful of legislative opponents filibustered legislation that would have allowed him to succeed himself. He boldly nominated his shy wife, Lurleen, to run as his stand-in. She obliterated a field of eight Democratic opponents and one hapless Republican. With Alabama safely under control and state contractors and suppliers pouring in seed money, the Wallace presidential campaign was under way by the fall of 1967.

There is no evidence that Wallace genuinely believed (despite his statements to the contrary) that he had a chance to win. His goals were to position himself for 1972 and, if the cards came up right, to throw the 1968 election into the House of Representatives. Even that possibility seemed farfetched in the fall of 1967. Polls showed his support to be nonexistent on the West Coast and in the Rocky Mountain states and less than 6 percent in the East and Midwest. Even on his home ground in the South, he would run a poor third to almost any Republican and Democratic candidates.[22]

Against all the odds, however, Wallace cobbled together the American

21. Los Angeles *Times,* July 2, 1966.
22. Mobile *Press Register,* September 10, 1967.

Independent Party and fought his way onto the ballots of all fifty states. Flying in an obsolete turboprop airplane, and with almost no professional advance staff, the candidate careened around the nation. Missed luggage, botched schedules, and failure to provide speech texts frustrated journalists, already angry that the Wallace plane was dry. But across the nation his support grew steadily through the spring and summer of 1968. Attacking Republicans and Democrats alike, he saved his choicest barbs for former vice-president Richard Nixon, who ultimately won his party's nomination. Nixon and the Republicans had been fighting for the "colored vote" since 1953, when Eisenhower had appointed Earl Warren to write the *Brown* v. *Board of Education* school decision, Wallace told the New York *Times*. "Nixon is just like the national Democrats. He's for all this Federal invasion of the states' right to run their own affairs." [23]

The war in Vietnam, a contributory factor to inflation and the economic slowdown of the 1960s and 1970s, fueled additional resentment, although its immediate political impact was cultural rather than economic. Despite the opportunity it offered for a crusade against godless Communism, the war itself was never very popular with Wallace supporters. Their quarrel was with the protest movement led by privileged elites (or, as Wallace called them, "silver-spooned brats") who rejected patriotism and a whole range of American cultural and religious values.[24]

The candidate seldom explicitly raised issues of race, but more fastidious political observers shuddered at his attacks on the federal courts for their busing orders, and his threats against "lawless street punks and demonstrators" repeatedly kindled the rage of his audiences.

George Wallace was one of the last grand masters of the kind of foot-stomping public speaking that characterized American politics—particularly southern American politics—in the age before television. Thousands of stump speeches, from county fairgrounds to Kiwanis Clubs, had given

---

23. New York *Times,* September 26, March 24, 1968.

24. Wallace and his followers had decidedly ambiguous views on Vietnam. He often urged more aggressive prosecution of the war, but as a group, Wallace voters in 1968 were much more likely to agree with the proposition that the United States should never have become involved in the conflict. See Seymour M. Lipset and Earl Raab, *The Politics of Unreason: Right-Wing Extremism in America, 1790–1970* (New York: Basic Books, 1970), 384–99.

him an unerring sense of what would "play." He was, in the vocabulary of the students of rhetoric, the perfect "mimetic orator," probing his audiences' fears and passions and articulating those emotions in a language and style they could understand.[25]

The issues might shift from state to state and region to region, but—whether he talked about busing, taxes, or prayer in the schools—George Wallace reached back to the language of his nineteenth-century Populist forebears as he celebrated the "producers" of American society: the "beauticians, the truck drivers, the office workers, the policemen and the small businessmen," who had formed the heart of the Democratic Party, "the bulk of its strength and vitality."

Wallace skillfully pulled from the American political fabric the strands of xenophobia, racism, and a "plain folk" cultural outlook that equated the cosmopolitan currents of the 1960s with moral corruption and weakness. His genius was his ability to voice his listeners' sense of betrayal—of victimhood—and to refocus their anger. Instead of the New York bankers and moneyed interests feared by his nineteenth-century counterparts, or the shadowy "Commies" of the McCarthy era, Wallace warned of the danger to the American soul posed by civil rights agitators and antiwar demonstrators who flaunted their contempt for the law and mocked patriotic and "Christian" values, by federal officials who threatened the property rights of homeowning Americans and the union seniority system of blue-collar workers, and by federal judges who protected the criminal and penalized the victim in their obsession with civil liberties.[26]

25. Despite the amateurish operation of his political campaigns, Wallace was no political Luddite as Marshall Frady suggests in his biography of the Alabama governor. Wallace paid close attention to political polling and adopted sophisticated computer mailings in order to build a political and financial base for his campaigns. Richard Viguerie, the father of ultra-right direct-mail fund-raising techniques, got his start with Wallace. See Nick Thimmesch, "The Grass-Roots Dollar Chase—Ready on the Right," *New York,* June 9, 1975, pp. 58–63.

26. Because of the Supreme Court's paramount role in challenging segregation in the 1950s and 1960s, it was an obvious target for Wallace the segregationist. What is striking, however, is the shift that took place after 1964 in Wallace's rhetoric. His attacks continued to have a racial theme (busing, early efforts at affirmative action, etc.), but much of his anger was focused on the Court's betrayal of "moral" and "traditional" values. Wallace talked as much about the Court's decision to outlaw school prayer as he did about its role in integrating public schools.

He might begin with abstract attacks on the "power of the central government," but he turned to earthy sarcasm as he sneered at the "so-called intelligentsia," the "intellectual snobs who don't know the difference between smut and great literature," the "hypocrites who send your kids half way across town while they have their chauffeur drop their children off at private schools," the "briefcase-carrying bureaucrats" who "can't even park their bicycles straight." [27] On paper his speeches are stunningly disconnected, even incoherent, but on flickering television screens and in giant political rallies he offered frightened and insecure millions a chance to strike back—if only rhetorically—at the enemy. To Hunter Thompson, the counterculture journalist who covered the 1968 and 1972 presidential campaigns, a Wallace performance was awe-inspiring, a political "Janis Joplin Concert." There was a sense, Thompson said "that the bastard had somehow levitated himself and was hovering over us." [28]

In the election of 1968, George Wallace became the voice of this political upheaval, and for a while it seemed that he would succeed in accomplishing his most ambitious goal: throwing the election into the House of Representatives. Through the summer and fall of 1968, the Harris and Gallup pollsters tracked Wallace's support as it grew from less than 10 percent in April, to 14 percent in mid-June, to 18 percent in mid-July, to 21 percent in late September. By October 1, a plurality—in some cases a majority—of Deep South voters supported the Alabama governor, who was also closing in on Nixon in Virginia, Tennessee, Kentucky, and Florida. Unmistakable polling evidence that Nixon was the second choice of 70 to 80 percent of the Wallace voters frustrated Republican campaign staffers. [29]

But Wallace's passionate support from his followers was not an unmixed blessing. As much religious exorcism as political exercise, the giant

27. Quotes are from Wallace's Op-Ed piece in the New York *Times,* March 1, 1972, and from the standard stump speech he repeated in the Florida campaign, as reported in the Birmingham *Post-Herald* and the Montgomery *Advertiser* in February and early March of 1972.

28. Hunter S. Thompson, *Fear and Loathing on the Campaign Trail '72* (San Francisco: Straight Arrow Books, 1973), 156.

29. Gallup, *Gallup Poll: 1935–1971,* III, 2099, 2130, 2134, 2139–41, 2143–54, 2163, 2167–69; Washington *Post,* September 17, 1968.

Wallace rallies revealed both his power and the limitations of that power. Few can match his appearance in Madison Square Garden on October 24, 1968. On an unusually warm fall evening in New York City, four hundred policemen—nearly a hundred on horseback—lined up on Seventh Avenue between West 31st and 33rd Streets as crowds began to pour into the city's largest indoor arena. Across the street an astonishing array of fringe groups gathered: a caravan of Ku Klux Klansmen from Louisiana; a delegation of followers of the "Minutemen of America" with neatly printed signs and armloads of brochures; a dozen jackbooted members of the American Nazi Party who sported swastika armbands and "I like Eich" buttons, worn in memory of Nazi war criminal Adolph Eichmann. New York police separated this motley crew from more than two hundred members of the Trotskyite Workers World Party and several hundred young people of the SDS who waved the black flag of anarchy. Altogether, more than two thousand black and white New Yorkers—most in their early twenties—brandished picket signs and shouted their conflicting chants. From the left: "Sieg Heil! Sieg Heil!" From the right: "Commie faggots! Commie faggots!"

By 8 P.M., 20,000 of the faithful, the largest indoor political gathering in New York City since a Franklin Roosevelt speech in 1936, packed the Garden. Wallace claimed the stage at 8:20. The audience erupted. Although the campaign had another week to run, for Wallace the rally was the emotional climax of his remarkable presidential race. Earlier in the summer he had drawn 70,000 supporters to the Boston Commons—more than any rally ever put on by the Kennedys, he constantly reminded reporters. In October he had spoken to crowds of 15,000 in Pittsburgh's Arena Auditorium, 16,000 at an outdoor rally in Baltimore, 12,000 in the San Francisco Cow Palace, 10,000 in the San Diego Sports Arena, 15,000 in Detroit's Cobo Hall, and 16,000 in Cincinnati's Convention Hall—all outside the South. And now 20,000 in the heartland of the enemy.[30]

While a brass band played a medley of patriotic songs, Wallace threw

30. Wallace claimed larger figures in almost every case in his campaign pamphlet *The George C. Wallace Presidential Campaign Souvenir Photo Album* (Selma, Ala.: Dallas Publishing Co., 1970). I have used the more conservative numbers furnished by police officials to the media.

kisses to a crowd that roared his name again and again in a chant audible to demonstrators outside the Garden and a half-block away. Curtis LeMay, his vice-presidential running mate, and LeMay's wife, Helen, joined him on the stage, but his supporters continued to whistle and shout. After more than fifteen minutes, Wallace managed to bring the crowd to order by having a country singer perform "God Bless America."

When Wallace finally spoke, he began awkwardly, seemingly over-whelmed by the fervor of his admirers. In the southwest balcony of the Garden, a squarely built black man stood and held up a poster proclaim-ing "Law and Order—Wallace Style." Underneath the slogan was the outline of a Ku Klux Klansman holding a noose. At his side, another demonstrator turned on a portable bullhorn and began shouting: "Wal-lace talks about law-and-order! Ask him what state has the highest murder rate! The most rapes! The most armed robberies!"

A squadron of police hurried toward the balcony to eject the hecklers as the crowd exploded in a rage that seemed to ignite the Alabama gov-ernor. "Why do the leaders of the two national parties kowtow to these anarchists?" he demanded, gesturing toward the protesters. "One of 'em laid down in front of President Johnson's limousine last year," he contin-ued with a snarl. "I tell you when November comes, the first time they lie down in front of my limousine it'll be the last one they'll ever lay down in front of; their day is *over!*"

The crowd leaped to its feet in the first of more than a half-dozen standing ovations and thirty interruptions for applause as Wallace poured out his proven applause lines. "We don't have a sick society, we have a sick Supreme Court," he said, as he scornfully described "perverted" de-cisions that disallowed prayer in the classrooms even as they defended the right to distribute "obscene pornography."

Fifteen minutes into his talk, he shed his jacket as he weaved and bobbed across the stage, his right fist clenched, his left jabbing out and down as if in the midst of a boxing match. "We don't have riots in Ala-bama," he shouted. "They start a riot down there, first one of 'em to pick up a brick gets a bullet in the brain, that's all. And then you walk over to the next one and say, 'All right, pick up a brick. We just want to see you pick up one of them bricks, now!'" [31]

31. New York *Post,* October 25, 1968; New York *Times,* October 25, 1968.

The crowd went berserk. Richard Strout, the genteel columnist of the *New Republic,* watched the spectacle that night with a mixture of fascination and horror. Never again, he told his readers, would he think about Germany in the 1930s without remembering this wild eruption of hatred.[32]

It is hardly a revelation to note the connection between power, politics, and sexuality. (In one of his stories of Washington politics and power, novelist Ward Just simply called it "the hots.") Wallace's appeal seemed to lurch uncertainly between eroticism and violence, closer to that of the "outlaw" country-music singer Waylon Jennings than to the suave John Kennedy whom the Alabama governor envied for his effortless grace. The energy flowed back and forth between Wallace and his audience in a performance that was palpably sexual, bizarrely blending the sacred—God, Mother, and Country—and the profane, with calls for violence and retribution, the damning of "the other."

Gerald Wallace bluntly acknowledged his brother's "mean streak." George was a first-rate amateur boxer, twice winning the state's Golden Gloves bantamweight championship. When he walked into the ring, the smiling, pleasant "old George" disappeared. He was "like an animal," a friend remembered uneasily. "Everybody's always trying to psychoanalyze George," his second wife, Cornelia, recalled in 1989. But if you "really want to understand him, just look at this." She held out a photograph of Wallace in a boxing ring, his face grimacing with concentration while he pummeled a blood-covered opponent.[33]

Wallace loved talking on the telephone or speaking to a crowd, Cornelia shrewdly observed, because there was always a safe distance between him and those who adored him. But her former husband could not tolerate genuine intimacy, she said. "He couldn't stand to get emotionally close to people." That was true with each of his three wives; it was equally true of his relationship with his children. Until the last few years, when he became reconciled with George Jr., Wallace had only the most superficial contacts with his son and his daughters. (It was years before George Jr. forgave his father for pressuring the dying Lurleen to run for governor in 1966.)[34]

---

32. "T.R.B. from Washington," *New Republic,* November 9, 1968, p. 4.
33. Author's interview with Cornelia Wallace, October 18, 1988.
34. "Daddy and I don't have time to share many activities," one of his daughters said

George Wallace never lost a political race in Alabama after 1958, but he came closest when he ran against Albert Brewer in 1970. Brewer, the faithful successor as governor to the late Mrs. Wallace, seemed just the ticket for a state temporarily sated with Wallace's political acrobatics. He almost eliminated Wallace from the campaign in the first primary in May and led by a wide margin going into the runoff. As the election drew near, however, one of Brewer's strongest supporters in eastern Alabama confided her fears of a Wallace victory to Anniston newspaper editor Brandt Ayers.

"Is it because of the race thing?" asked Ayers, in a reference to Wallace's attacks on Brewer as the tool of the black vote.

No, the woman replied, and she spread her thumb and pointer finger an inch apart: "The problem is that the voters think that Albert has a tee-tee about this long." [35]

Crude, certainly—but the off-color observation accurately captured the musky chauvinism that characterized George Wallace's political identity.

Journalists of the time marveled at Wallace's ability to transcend his southern roots by appealing to working-class voters outside the region. What they seldom observed, however, were the particular contours of that appeal. Wallace as the pugnacious southern bad boy drew his support heavily from young white men between the ages of eighteen and thirty-five. As late as three weeks before the election of 1968, he outdrew Humphrey *and* Nixon in that segment of the voting population.[36] The basic bond between Wallace and his audience was the ethos of the locker room, of a man's world free from the constraints of women and their weaknesses. In the 1960s, rage was, after all, still a male prerogative.

---

in an unguarded interview as she described a father distant and uninvolved even after her mother died. Birmingham *News,* October 27, 1968. George Wallace Jr. is dutifully loyal to his father in his account *The Wallaces of Alabama,* but the thread that runs throughout the book is one of a son isolated from a man far too concerned with collecting votes to be a father. (The book opens with an unconsciously revealing description of a near-death experience by George Jr. at age twenty-one. As he fought a Gulf Coast undertow, his only concern was how much he had loved his father and how he had failed to accomplish enough in his young life to earn his father's pride and love in return.)

35. Brandt Ayers, APT Interview.
36. *The Gallup Opinion Index,* June 1972, Report No. 84.

Alienated Americans who mobbed Wallace at his rallies or cheered his television performances were thrilled at having found a champion. Still, what most American voters—even many of the Wallace voters—wanted was a return to a time of safety and stability, not a program of unending struggle. As the campaign of 1968 drew to a close, it was clear that George Wallace had been the first politician to sense and then to exploit the changes America came to know by many names: white backlash, the silent majority, the alienated voters. His threatening demeanor and fiery personality would limit him to the role of redneck poltergeist, but as George Wallace neared the limits of his political popularity, he opened the door for his successors to manipulate and exploit the politics of anger.

2 | THE POLITICS OF ACCOMMODATION

By the summer of 1968, almost eight years after his loss to John Kennedy and six years after Pat Brown trounced him in his campaign for the California governorship, Richard Nixon had nearly completed his own Long March to the presidency. During those years of exile, American politics had been turned upside down. The assassinations of John Kennedy and Martin Luther King, the race riots of the mid-1960s, the escalation of the war in Vietnam, and the explosion of the antiwar movement had created a whole new constellation of issues. In the first six months of 1968, Eugene McCarthy had driven Lyndon Johnson from seeking a second term, then Robert Kennedy had surged forward as the Democratic front-runner, only to be gunned down in California. Hubert Humphrey had accepted the Democratic nomination at a convention spoiled by riots in Chicago's streets and bitter divisiveness within his own party. Pollsters gave Nixon a twenty-point lead over his Democratic opponent. Even before the debacle in Chicago, Nixon's acclamation by a united Republican convention in Miami seemed more a coronation than the opening round of a presidential campaign.

At his West Coast retreat at Mission Bay, California, Nixon and his staff spent the week after the convention planning fund raising for the coming months and surveying the issues they believed would dominate the coming race: the war in Vietnam abroad; inflation and the growing spiral of civic disobedience and racial conflict at home. The nominee very early made the decision to follow the classic course of the front-runner.

He would propose no substantive (and high-risk) policies. Franklin Roosevelt had adopted much the same approach in his 1932 campaign against Hoover, as had Thomas Dewey in his run against Truman in 1948. But in this new age of media consciousness, the Nixon staff was much more calculating in its attempt to craft the shape of the campaign. Through a vast and enormously complex daily polling operation carried out by Princeton's Opinion Research Corporation, the Republican high command tracked the mood of the electorate in fourteen key states and advised Nixon on how to adjust his daily rhetoric to defuse the "negatives" as the pollsters defined them.

In June of 1967, H. R. Haldeman had prepared a memorandum that laid out the critical role television would play in the reemergence of Nixon. Rallies and repeated exposure to opponents' supporters ("and paid troublemakers") were counterproductive. The time had come for political campaigning to "move out of the dark ages and into the brave new world of the omnipresent eye."[1] Haldeman apparently did not grasp the implications of the snippets he had borrowed from the bleak prophecies of Aldous Huxley and George Orwell in their anti-utopian novels. (In his 1934 novel *Brave New World,* Huxley satirized a totalitarian future in which society disregarded individual dignity and worshiped science and the machine. In Orwell's even bleaker satire *Nineteen Eighty-four,* published in 1949, the omnipresent eye was that of Big Brother—the government—peering into every aspect of citizens' lives via two-way television.)

If they were a little weak on Western literature, Nixon's men knew the tools of their trade. Television would allow minimum uncontrolled exposure of the candidate and an opportunity for maximum manipulation of the electorate. As one of Nixon's media advisers told him even before his nomination: "Voters are basically lazy, basically uninterested in making an *effort* to understand what we're talking about. . . . Reason requires a high degree of discipline, of concentration. . . . The emotions are more easily roused, closer to the surface, more malleable. . . . It's the aura that surrounds the charismatic figure more than it is the figure itself, that draws the followers. Our task is to build that aura."[2]

1. Richard Nixon, *The Memoirs of Richard Nixon* (New York: Grosset & Dunlap, 1978), 303.

2. Joe McGinniss, *The Selling of the President, 1968* (New York: Trident Press, 1969), 36–37.

Nixon's chief speechwriter, Raymond Price, was even more explicit. For most voters, he said, the decision to support a candidate was a "gut reaction, unarticulated, non-analytical, a product of the particular chemistry between the voter and the *image* of the candidate." It's "not what's *there* that counts, its what's projected." And this projection "depends more on the medium and its use than it does on the candidate himself."[3] The slogan "Nixon's the One" would emphasize the campaign's focus on Nixon as the alternative to the failed policies of the past. John Mitchell would be in charge of the Republican effort, but Harry Treleaven, the venture's advertising director, would act as field commander—with a force of ninety advance men and public relations specialists—to choreograph the movements of Nixon, Agnew, and the half-dozen star surrogate speakers. Television appearances would provide opportunities to wrap the candidate in a carefully crafted aura of warmth, competence, and invincible success. As Nixon confided to Haldeman, the first thing to do was establish the "Churchill analogy." He would "play the confident line from now until November. . . . We should exude confidence, not cockiness."[4] The Nixon team would labor without ceasing to avoid a campaign of raucous debates and alternative policies. They would create—in Joe McGinniss' memorable metaphor—a campaign that was the political equivalent of an indoor stadium "where the wind would never blow, the temperature never rise or fall, and the ball never bounce erratically on the artificial grass." Just as John Kennedy had molded a public's image of Camelot on the Potomac, Nixon would shape the nation's perception of him as a great and compassionate leader.[5]

Alas, poor Richard! Kennedy's skills as a television performer had made it possible to conceal his administration's self-conscious manipulation of the media. Each time Nixon, anxious to appear natural and likable, to seem to be in command, stepped onto a stage or before a television camera, voters—and viewers—always had an uneasy sense that machinery was rolling vast stage sets into place, that stagehands were scurrying

3. *Ibid.*, 38–39.
4. Stephen E. Ambrose, *Nixon: The Triumph of a Politician, 1962–1972* (New York: Simon & Schuster, 1989), 180–81, Vol. II of Ambrose, *Nixon,* 3 vols.
5. McGinniss, *Selling of the President, 1968,* p. 39.

around just off-camera, that makeup had been painstakingly applied for the evening performance. Remembering his ill-fated debates with John Kennedy, Nixon vacillated in making an all-out commitment to television. Perhaps he sensed that the all-seeing eye would simply confirm ad man Roger Ailes's devastating description: that when other kids got footballs for Christmas, Richard Nixon was the boy who got a briefcase—and loved it. Still, by the beginning of his presidency, he had embraced the main lessons taught by his Madison Avenue handlers. His staff, he told Haldeman at one point, was spending far too much time worrying about his position on issues rather than shaping his "public appearance—presence." Whenever possible he should be presented to a "naive type audience," specifically, "no Jewish groups." The important thing to remember, he concluded, was that "speech is obsolete as a means of communication."[6]

Nixon had begun shaping his political strategy for 1968 after the Goldwater fiasco. Capturing the South was the linchpin of his plan. The notion that Goldwater had started the Southern Strategy was so much "bullshit," Nixon would later insist; it was Eisenhower who had campaigned in the South in 1952 and 1956, making dramatic inroads and drawing support from both the old Dixiecrats and an emerging middle-class constituency more in tune with traditional Republican economic conservatism than old-style racism. By 1964, however, the civil rights movement had galvanized angry whites within the region, nowhere more intensely than in the Deep South. Goldwater had been drawn to that constituency like a moth to a flame. As a result, Nixon later concluded, he "ran as a racist candidate . . . and he won the wrong [southern] states": Mississippi, Georgia, Alabama, Louisiana, and South Carolina.[7] With that political shrewdness that seldom failed him, Nixon saw that Goldwater's decision to identify with what one aide called the "foam-at-the-mouth segregationists" weakened Republicans' appeals to moderates in the border states and in the North. That was one reason Nixon chose Spiro Agnew of Maryland as his running mate. Initially the Maryland governor was widely regarded as a

6. *Ibid.,* 103; H. R. Haldeman notes of meetings with RN, March 15, 1970, Box 41, H. R. Haldeman Papers, Richard Nixon Presidential Materials, National Archives, College Park, Md. (hereinafter cited as RNPM).

7. Transcript of interview between Herbert Parmet and Richard Nixon, November 16, 1988. Copy in possession of author.

moderate, but Nixon deployed him as a surrogate Wallace. The Deep South could be counted on to come home to the Republicans because the national Democratic Party—with its sensitivity to its black constituency— did not offer a viable alternative.

Harry Dent, a former aide to Strom Thurmond and one of the principal architects of the Southern Strategy, repeatedly insisted that neither that strategy nor the GOP candidate's generally conservative emphasis in 1968 was racist. And, in fact, he (like other members of the Nixon team) scrupulously avoided explicit references to race. The problem with the liberalism of the Democrats, Dent charged, was not that it was too pro-black; its real failure was that it had created an America in which the streets were "filled with radical dissenters, cities were literally burning down, crime seemed uncontrollable," and vast social programs were creating a class of the permanently dependent even as they bankrupted the middle class. The rising tide of economic and social conservatism clearly complemented opposition to federal activism, North and South. But it was disingenuous to argue (as did Dent and other practitioners of the Southern Strategy) that race was irrelevant; the political driving force of Nixon's policies toward the South was seldom simply an abstract notion about the "preservation of individual freedom."[8]

In reality, almost every issue in the campaign was tightly interwoven with issues of race. In 1968 the American economy was drawing near the end of a remarkable quarter-century of sustained growth and rising wages across the income spectrum. Between 1947 and 1965, the purchasing power of middle-class and lower-middle-class workers rose an average of more than 2 percent per year. But that steady ascension had begun to slow in the late 1960s. Between 1965 and 1968, a combination of accelerating price increases and sharp hikes in payroll and income taxes led to a near stagnation in real wages for the average blue-collar and salaried white-collar worker. Family income remained stable and even rose slightly, but primarily because of the movement of women into the work force. Families were working harder in order to stay in place.

Higher taxes and the first wave of inflation generated by the Vietnam

8. Harry S. Dent, *The Prodigal South Returns to Power* (New York: Wiley, 1978), 75–76.

War also affected black and Hispanic Americans; nevertheless, nonwhites made remarkable economic as well as political gains through the 1960s. It would become an accepted truism that the Civil Rights Acts of the 1960s primarily benefited upwardly mobile and middle-class blacks. In reality, there were significant increases for working-class blacks as well. Between 1961 and 1968, total "aggregate" income for whites increased 56 percent, while the total for nonwhites went up 110 percent. Most of that increase stemmed from an upgrading in occupations as black Americans—particularly in the South—commanded higher-wage jobs. During these same years, the antipoverty and social welfare programs of the Kennedy and Johnson administrations transferred approximately $121 billion to individuals living below the poverty line; over 30 percent of those funds went to black Americans. Had that amount been retained by white Americans in low- and middle-income brackets, it would have added less than three-eighths of 1 percent to their actual disposable income. But that was not the public perception. The slowdown in the rate of economic growth surprised a white working class accustomed to a steadily rising standard of living. The poor—particularly the black poor—became increasingly appealing scapegoats.[9]

Issues of race were interwoven with concerns over social disorder in American streets. At a Wallace rally or a Nixon appearance, the distinction between antiwar and civil rights demonstrators, between heckling protesters and street muggers, seemed almost nonexistent. In the minds of many of Nixon's listeners—and in Nixon's mind, however often he denied it—race and disorder were always linked. And occasionally his facade

9. The literature on income, poverty, and the impact of governmental tax structure and transfer programs is complex and often contradictory. Perhaps the most useful information I have found lies in Edward C. Budd, ed., *Inequality and Poverty* (New York: W. W. Norton, 1967); Sheldon Danziger and Kent Portney, *The Distributional Impacts of Public Policies* (New York: St. Martin, 1988); Robert Haveman, *Starting Even: An Equal Opportunity Program to Combat the Nation's New Poverty* (New York: Simon & Schuster, 1988); Edgar K. Browning, *Redistribution and the Welfare System* (Washington, D.C.: American Enterprise Institute, 1975); Andrew F. Brimmer, "Inflation and Income Distribution in the United States," *Review of Economics and Statistics,* LIII (February 1971), 37–48; S. M. Miller, "Sharing the Burden of Change," in *The White Majority: Between Poverty and Affluence,* ed. Louise Kapp Howe (New York: Random House, 1970), 279–93.

slipped. On one occasion early in the campaign, he taped a television commercial attacking the decline of "law and order" in American cities. Viewing the finished product, an unguarded Nixon became more expansive with his staff. The commercial "hits it right on the nose," he said enthusiastically. "It's all about law and order and the damn Negro–Puerto Rican groups out there." Nixon did not have to mention race any more than did Ronald Reagan when he began one of his famous discourses on welfare queens using food stamps to buy porterhouse steaks; the audience was already primed to make that connection. (As longtime Nixon aide John Ehrlichman would later acknowledge, his boss genuinely believed that blacks could only "marginally benefit from Federal programs because blacks were *genetically inferior* to whites.")[10]

For nearly a hundred years after the Civil War, the racial phobias of white southern Democrats had been used to maintain a solid Democratic South. To Nixon, it seemed poetic justice that the tables should be turned. The trick lay in sympathizing with and appealing to the fears of angry whites without appearing to become an extremist and driving away moderates—or, as Ehrlichman described the process, to present a position on crime, education, or public housing in such a way that a voter could "avoid admitting to himself that he was attracted by a racist appeal."[11]

Such tactics were not reserved for southern whites. Measuring national attitudes on race is notoriously difficult; even the increasing sophistication of polling in the 1950s and 1960s often failed to distinguish between momentary responses to headline-grabbing racial incidents and long-term attitudinal changes. If the shape and dimensions of a white backlash were still unclear, however, it required no great political insight to detect the emergence of that white political undertow. The work of pollsters Louis Harris, George Gallup, the Roper Research Associates, and the University of Michigan Survey Research Center simply documented what dozens of contemporary reporters and political leaders sensed: the growing hostility to the gains made by the civil rights movement and the intention to resist further civil rights gains.[12] The race riots of 1966 and 1967 and the in-

10. McGinniss, *Selling of the President, 1968,* p. 23; John Ehrlichman, *Witness to Power: The Nixon Years* (New York: Simon & Schuster, 1982), 223.

11. Ehrlichman, *Witness to Power,* 223.

12. See, for example, the series of surveys of racial attitudes edited by Hazel Erskine and

creasing federal pressure to integrate northern schools and housing made it apparent that capital could be made among discontented white Democrats in the North as well as in the South. The task for Nixon was to move just to the right of a Democratic Party that had to be mindful of its black constituency. Complicating the process was the fact that the GOP candidate genuinely wanted to avoid a divisive presidential campaign. This desire did not stem from any concern over polarizing the American electorate; rather—in 1968, at least—Nixon had great ambitions for his presidency in domestic as well as foreign affairs. He believed a bitter campaign would make his task more difficult.

At least as early as 1966, Nixon had grasped the threat that George Wallace posed to his personal political future and to the fortunes of the Republican Party. On one of his many fund-raising tours—generating IOUs for the 1968 campaign—Nixon stopped off in South Carolina for a rally and benefit for Strom Thurmond and the state's emerging Republican Party. Thurmond's aide Harry Dent drove Nixon to the airport. His passenger made no attempt to be coy. "I'm running for the presidency," he announced. And while he had no illusions about the difficulties of getting the nomination and defeating Johnson (who he assumed would run for reelection), George Wallace was his greatest barrier to election. If Wallace should "take most of the South," Nixon would be "unable to win enough votes in the rest of the country to gain a clear majority." Either Johnson would win outright or the election would go into the Democrat-controlled House of Representatives. Wallace, Nixon concluded intensely, was the key to his chances for winning the presidency.[13]

By late summer, 1968, Johnson was no longer a candidate. Polls showed Nixon leading a battered Humphrey by as many as twenty points. But, with memories of his cliffhanger defeat in 1960, Nixon was convinced that the race would be much closer.

He was right. Wallace climbed steadily in the polls to claim more than

---

published in 1967 and 1968 in *Public Opinion Quarterly:* "The Polls: Negro Housing" (Fall, 1967), 482–98; "The Polls: Demonstrations and Race Riots" (Winter, 1967–68), 655–67; "The Polls: Negro Employment" (Spring, 1968), 132–53; and "The Polls: Speed of Racial Integration" (Fall, 1968), 513–24.

13. Dent, *Prodigal South,* 77; Author's interview with Harry Dent, July 20, 1988.

20 percent of the electorate. Almost imperceptibly, disgruntled Democrats outside the South began to abandon their tentative allegiance to the GOP and to return to the party of their fathers. By the last week in September, Nixon still had a ten-point lead, but it was shrinking week by week. Wallace's strong position in the South revived the growing possibility that Humphrey might squeak through with a narrow victory, or—as Wallace had hoped—the election might be thrown into the House.

Capturing a majority of the southern electoral votes became a matter of survival for Nixon. He could not be certain whether Wallace helped or hurt him in the heartland states of the Midwest; one poll suggested that a majority of Wallace supporters outside the South would—if forced to choose—pick Humphrey over Nixon by a narrow margin. Another named Nixon as the second choice of the majority of northern Wallace voters. But the pollsters were consistent in their finding that the Republican was the second choice of 80 percent of Wallace voters in the South. How could he strip away these southern voters? That was proving more difficult than Nixon had imagined, particularly since he wanted to run a nondivisive campaign.

Nixon himself conceived the counterattack against the Alabama challenger, but maneuvers were directed by Harry Dent, who took charge of an ostensibly independent southern operation for the general election with the unlikely title "Thurmond Speaks for Nixon-Agnew." Dent coordinated strategy with the GOP campaign and in fact cleared every major decision through John Mitchell, although a wary Nixon never officially brought Dent on board his team.

Nowhere was Nixon's caution more evident than in his handling of the critical question of desegregation. In the mid- and late 1960s, southern school districts had resisted court-ordered desegregation with a variety of so-called freedom of choice plans, which placed the burden of desegregation upon black parents (since it seemed apparent that most whites would not choose to send their children to black schools). "Freedom of choice" became a popular rallying cry, suggesting grass-roots democracy—the right of parents to choose—and neutrality on the question of race. Of course, everyone knew that freedom of choice plans minimized comprehensive desegregation.

To southern Republicans, it was obvious that most white Americans—

North and South—were increasingly opposed to the Johnson administration's attempts to bring about significant desegregation of the schools. By September, Nixon's running mate, Agnew, was in full-throated pursuit of the Democrats as the party of treason abroad and permissiveness at home, but neither he nor Nixon made more than the vaguest response to southern Republicans' pleas that the campaign commit itself to stopping (or dramatically slowing) the pace of desegregation in the South.

In mid-September, as he watched his southern base erode under attacks from Wallace, Nixon agreed to an interview with two Charlotte television newsmen. In a carefully planned trial balloon, the GOP nominee endorsed freedom of choice plans and attacked mandated desegregation plans. Placing "slum"—*i.e.,* predominantly black—children in schools in wealthier areas was counterproductive, he declared, because "they are two or three grades behind and all you do is destroy their ability to compete." Without explicitly endorsing freedom of choice plans, he made clear (he thought) his opposition to busing. But the shift in his position on this sensitive issue was so subtle it passed unnoticed by the press. A frustrated Dent wanted to use excerpts from the interview in televised advertisements to drive home Nixon's new stance, but the former vice-president, fearful of the political fallout, hesitated for more than three weeks. In the end, he decided to take the risk. On October 7, in an interview with UPI editors in Washington, he reiterated his opposition to "forced busing" and his support for freedom of choice plans. When Humphrey spoke to the same editors two days later and attacked freedom of choice plans as a "subterfuge for segregation," Dent moved into action and began to place regional ads comparing the two candidates' positions.[14]

14. Charlotte *Observer,* September 13, 1968; Dent, *Prodigal South,* 111–14. The willingness to embrace freedom of choice was part of a larger mood of anxiety in the Nixon campaign. The same week that Dent began using the ads dramatizing Nixon's opposition to court-ordered desegregation, the Republicans aired a savage commercial that included a montage of photographs juxtaposing images of a grinning Hubert Humphrey with urban race riots and wounded and dying soldiers in Vietnam. By comparison, the Democrats' 1964 anti-Goldwater "daisy" commercial, suggesting that the election of the Republican might bring nuclear war, was a masterpiece of subtlety. Kathleen Hall Jamieson, *Packaging the Presidency: A History and Criticism of Presidential Campaign Advertising* (New York: Oxford University Press, 1992), 244.

At the same time, Dent's careful polling in the South revealed Wallace's Achilles' heel: the fear of angry white southerners that a vote for the Alabama governor would allow Humphrey to win the election. Thurmond's aide put together a commercial in which country-music star Stuart Hamblen sang a sad song of southerners who were chasing a rabbit—George Wallace—while the real enemy of the South, Hubert Humphrey, waltzed into the White House. Dent and several southerners on the Republican team urged that the Nixon campaign buy up blocks of advertising on southern country-music stations, particularly slots on the Wally Fowler Gospel Hour and the popular shows hosted by Buck Owens, Ernest Tubb, and the Wilburn Brothers. Publicity director Harry Treleaven and the advertising wizards at Fuller, Smith and Ross recoiled in horror, but South Carolina textile industrialist Roger Milliken, whose long career as a union buster had given him a finely honed sense of his workers' *mentalité,* did not have to be persuaded. Within twenty-four hours, he and four fellow textile magnates raised sufficient money to enlist Roy Acuff, Tex Ritter, and Stuart Hamblen in Dent's down-home campaign.[15]

Nixon himself took to the airwaves across the region to drive home his message the last week of the campaign. "There's been a lot of double-talk about the role of the South in the campaign of nineteen sixty-eight, and I think it's time for some straight talk," he declared. The people of the South—by which he meant most of the white people of the South—would vote three to one against Humphrey if given the option, he earnestly told his audience. Without mentioning Wallace by name, he warned that a "divided vote" would play into the hands of the Humphrey Democrats. "And so I say," he concluded, "don't play their game. Don't divide your vote. Vote for . . . the only team that can provide the new leadership that American needs, the Nixon-Agnew team. And I pledge to you we will restore law and order in this country."[16]

The Nixon strategy worked, in part because the Wallace campaign had

15. Dent, *Prodigal South,* 110–11; McGinniss, *Selling of the President, 1968,* pp. 122–23; Author's interview with Harry Dent, July 20, 1988.

16. McGinniss, *Selling of the President, 1968,* p. 21. In her study of presidential campaign advertising since the 1950s, Kathleen Hall Jamieson—who apparently looked only at the Treleaven campaign ads—erroneously suggests that Nixon did not use this argument in his campaign advertising. Jamieson, *Packaging the Presidency,* 233.

suffered a number of self-inflicted wounds, the greatest of which was the Alabamian's disastrous choice of retired Air Force general Curtis ("Bombs Away") LeMay as his running mate. Like a stuck phonograph needle, LeMay kept returning to his favorite subject: Americans' "irrational" fear of nuclear weapons (Hubert Humphrey began referring gleefully to the Wallace-LeMay ticket as "the Bombsey Twins"). By election day the Wallace candidacy—like most third-party movements—had faltered. Nevertheless, one of every eight voters supported him, and he showed surprising strength outside his own region. In addition to the five southern states he carried, Wallace polled from 8 to 15 percent of the vote in eighteen nonsouthern states. A statistically insignificant shift of votes in Tennessee and the two Carolinas and a 1 percent increase in the Democratic vote in Ohio and New Jersey would indeed have thrown the election into the House of Representatives.[17]

It was a close call, and it did not bode well for the future majority Richard Nixon hoped to build. The most salient figures that emerged following the 1968 election came from pollsters Richard Scammon and Ben Wattenberg: four of every five Wallace voters in the South, and slightly more than three of every five in the North, would have voted for Nixon with Wallace out of the contest.[18]

Richard Nixon began to plan his reelection campaign in the first weeks after Inauguration Day. It is tempting to read history backwards, to strip away the awkward stops, starts, and detours of Nixon's policies as he sought to evolve a political strategy that would bring Wallace voters into the Republican Party yet would not make Nixon appear to capitulate to the darker side of the third-party movement. If there is one thing that is clear from the history of the Nixon years, it is the absence of any ideological dogmatism.

17. Nor was that the only permutation for an election debacle. In Ohio and New Jersey, where Nixon squeaked by Humphrey, Wallace faded badly in the week preceding the election and, in those states, almost 60 percent of the last-minute voter switch was from Wallace to Humphrey. An additional 2-percent shift of Wallace voters to Humphrey would have had the same disastrous results for Nixon by throwing Ohio and New Jersey into the Democratic column and blocking a Nixon majority in the electoral college.

18. Richard M. Scammon and Ben J. Wattenberg, *The Real Majority: How the Silent Center of the American Electorate Chooses Its President* (New York: Coward-McCann & Geoghegan, 1970), 182–83.

During his first year in office, the president sent out a steady stream of mixed signals on racial issues. Addressing a group of southern congressmen and senators, he declared himself in favor of desegregation but against integration, a semantic distinction that apparently meant he was against segregation in theory but opposed to any policies that would actually bring about a mixing of the races in schools or neighborhoods.[19] Despite such rhetorical assurances to opponents of desegregation, Nixon appointed his relatively liberal friend Robert Finch as secretary of health, education and welfare, and Finch in turn supported the aggressive team of civil rights enforcers he had inherited from the Johnson administration.

Despite his obsession with winning the next election and his private feelings on the issue of race, Nixon drew—however hazily—a line between the politics of getting elected and the politics of governing during his first two years in office. That meant a need to "do something" about the increasing racial polarization of American society. In that process he was critically influenced by Daniel Patrick Moynihan, an ambitious young politician—a Democrat, of all things, but a neoconservative Democrat—who proved to be a master at finding common ground with the Republican president.[20]

Moynihan had been a reformer within the New York Democratic Party in the 1950s and was that rare blend of political operative and scholar intellectual, the professorial politician. By the end of the decade he was widely recognized as one of the most astute observers of the problems of America's urban scene. Through the 1960s, his allegiance shifted from John Kennedy to Lyndon Johnson to Robert Kennedy before settling for an extended rest in the Nixon administration.

At first glance it seemed an odd arrangement: the brooding partisan Nixon and the ebullient Irish American Moynihan. Although it is tempting to see the Democrat's alliance with Nixon as a matter of pure self-interest, well before the 1968 election he had begun to question some of the assumptions of Lyndon Johnson's Great Society. In particular, the vitriolic response to his 1965 report on the black family had made him

19. Harry Dent Memo, August 6, 1970, in Dent Papers, RNPM.
20. Herbert S. Parmet, *Richard Nixon and His America* (Boston: Little, Brown & Co., 1990), 546.

more willing to weigh his traditional allegiance.[21] In a 1967 speech entitled "The Politics of Stability," Moynihan set forth three propositions:

First, Democratic liberals had to "see more clearly that their essential interest is in the stability of the social order." They should reject the fringe elements within their party and move toward a coalition with responsible conservatives who shared a concern over social disorder and division.

Second, liberals should abandon their blind faith in the notion that the federal government was the most suitable vehicle for ameliorating social problems. Conservatives had a point in arguing that the national government was too distant and too out of touch with local problems to bring about effective change. Instead, Moynihan proposed the decentralization of social welfare programs whenever possible by giving state and local governments increased resources through revenue sharing.

Third, liberals had to stop "defending and explaining away" the problems in the black community as nothing more than the product of racism. Although rather vague, Moynihan's comments clearly hearkened back to the uproar that had greeted his report on instability within the black family. He continued to believe that drastic action had to be taken to prevent what he saw as the deterioration of the black family and the rise of welfare dependency.[22]

The speech did not mark the abandonment of Moynihan's principles or goals. In a magazine article printed that same year, he insisted that he had never implied that racism and its legacy were insignificant. "You do not take a person who for years has been hobbled by chains and liberate him, bring him up to the starting line of a race and then say, 'You are free to compete with all the others,' and still justly believe that you have been completely fair." On the other hand, said Moynihan, the nation could "simply not afford the luxury of having a large lower class that is at once deviant and dependent." If the crisis of race relations was to be resolved, it meant lowering the rhetoric and placing the problems of black

21. For the background on the controversy over the black family and Moynihan's response, see Lee Rainwater and William L. Yancey, *The Moynihan Report and the Politics of Controversy* (Cambridge, Mass.: Massachusetts Institute of Technology Press, 1967), and Daniel P. Moynihan, *Maximum Feasible Misunderstanding* (New York: Free Press, 1969).

22. Daniel P. Moynihan, "The Politics of Stability," *New Leader,* October 9, 1967.

Americans in the larger context of supporting lower-income families across the board.[23]

Moynihan's 1967 speech and article caught Richard Nixon's attention and led to their first meeting, in Key Biscayne, Florida, shortly after the election. They hit it off immediately, and—despite Moynihan's many sardonic comments on old friends and enemies—Nixon always retained his fondness for the Irishman.[24]

Even before Nixon took the oath of office, Moynihan laid out an agenda for action in the field of race relations. Skillfully, he played to the president-elect's contempt for the welfare bureaucracy by scathingly attacking social workers, urban planners, and a welfare establishment that he characterized as a grasping corps of middle-class apparatchiks who, intent on survival, nurtured the politics of resentment.

The solution, said Moynihan, was not to abandon the poor but to bypass the parasitic and wasteful bureaucracy through a guaranteed family income. (He was not alone in suggesting such a measure, but he was clearly the key figure in persuading Nixon to support a proposal backed by only a small minority within the leadership of the new administration.) In August of 1969, in a major televised address on domestic legislation, Nixon announced his proposal for a Family Assistance Plan, a nationalized welfare program that would offer a minimum standard of living in return for a work commitment. Payments would not go just to families with fatherless children, but to families with fathers living at home. The existing welfare system destabilized families by rewarding single motherhood, reinforcing dependency, and penalizing those who struggled to maintain the traditional family unit. By establishing automated payment procedures similar to Social Security, Nixon explained, the FAP would drastically reduce costs and would phase out many of the social workers and personnel who had profited from the old welfare system.

The Family Assistance Plan was not the only measure proposed by Nixon to deal with the problem of black poverty. During his first year in

---

23. Daniel P. Moynihan, "The President and the Negro: The Moment Lost," *Commentary,* February 1967. Both Moynihan speeches are reprinted in his collection of essays and speeches *Coping: On the Practice of Government* (New York: Random House, 1973).

24. Nixon, *Memoirs,* 341–42.

office, he created the Office of Minority Enterprises to promote black capitalism and backed the beginning of so-called set-aside programs, which required that a fixed percentage of government contracts be guaranteed to minority businesses. And through the Department of Labor, the Nixon administration instituted the so-called Philadelphia Plan, which required companies doing business with the federal government to establish goals and timetables for hiring and promotion—even if such procedures meant interference with longtime seniority practices.[25]

But the centerpiece of the Nixon program was the Family Assistance Plan, and it was a bold measure by any standard. By the administration's own numbers, the FAP would add from 10 million to 13 million Americans—no one was exactly certain—to the nation's welfare rolls. Even under the most optimistic projections, welfare costs would increase by $4 billion during the first year, with unknown costs in future years. The gamble was worth attempting in the hope of stabilizing the condition of the nation's poor, particularly the black poor. (Although the administration never released the figures, one study showed that the plan would have a particularly powerful impact on southern blacks, increasing benefits by 40 percent within the fourteen states of the region.)

In the end, the FAP stalled in Congress. Nixon, pointing to the opposition of professional welfare workers and radical groups such as the National Welfare Rights Organization, tended to blame liberals for the opposition to the program. In fact, there was little enthusiasm within his own cabinet or among Republican conservatives, the powerful United States Chamber of Commerce came out in bitter opposition, and a handful of key liberals were uneasy over the workfare provisions of the program. But the real problem lay in the new political equation.[26]

The year 1970 marked a critical turning point for the Nixon administration. The full dimensions of the political shift of 1968 were increasingly clear in the postmortems of the political analysts. In *Harper's Magazine, Atlantic, New York,* and in the leading newspapers of the nation, there

25. The best description of these programs can be found in Hugh Davis Graham, *The Civil Rights Era: Origins and Development of National Policy, 1960–1972* (New York: Oxford University Press, 1990).

26. Parmet, *Richard Nixon,* 549–61; Ambrose, *Nixon: The Triumph of a Politician,* 293–94, 345, 366–67, 402–406, 657–58.

was a new tone. Liberal columnist Pete Hamill, a son of the white working class, wrote eloquently of the "revolt of the white lower-middle class"— the social tier of what Peter Schrag labeled "the forgotten American."[27] Meanwhile, four quite disparate authors—Kevin Phillips, Richard Scammon, Ben Wattenberg, and Samuel Lubell—did as much as anyone to clarify the role of George Wallace in illuminating the changes that had taken place at the end of the 1960s. Their books, all published within a matter of months in late 1969 and early 1970, became more than simply accounts of these changes; they became part of the story.

Richard Scammon and Ben Wattenberg were the most self-consciously moderate and "middle of the road" of the group. Their message was simple: the Democratic Party had lost touch with the mainstream of the American electorate, which was white, middle-aged, and middle class. George Wallace had it right, they argued, when he railed against "pseudo-intellectuals" and journalists who were always "looking down their noses at the average man on the street, the glassworker, the steelworker, the autoworker and the textile worker, the farmer, the policeman, the beautician and the barber and the little businessman." Although they did not coin the term, Scammon and Wattenberg popularized a catchphrase that would soon become a staple of the political lexicon: *social issues.* Most critical, they suggested, was a belief that American society faced a crisis that went beyond the rise of street crime and social unrest, the breakdown of "law and order," to include the disintegration of the very cultural values that underlay the social system.[28]

Unfortunately, Scammon and Wattenberg argued, the Democratic Party's "pro-black stance" and refusal to take a hard-line attitude toward antiwar protesters and demonstrators linked it to the losing side of the emerging social issues. The party might continue its social welfare traditions in modified form, but it must stop scolding Americans about the restrictions of the Bill of Rights and take a tough line opposing crime

27. Pete Hamill, "The Revolt of the White Lower-Middle Class," *New York,* April 14, 1969, pp. 28–47; Marshall Frady, "Gary, Indiana," *Harper's Magazine* (August 1969), 35–45; Peter Schrag, "The Forgotten American," *Harper's Magazine* (August 1969), 27–34. *Newsweek* devoted almost an entire issue in the fall of 1969 to "The Troubled American: A Special Report on the White Majority." *Newsweek,* October 6, 1969, pp. 28–73.

28. Scammon and Wattenberg, *Real Majority,* 62, 96–100, 166–68, 284–86.

in the streets, campus disruptions, drugs, and pornography. Above all else, they insisted, the party had to disentangle these issues from that of race.[29]

There was a certain deceptive appeal to such a prescription. Too many exhibitionists in the Democratic leadership equated egocentric proclamations with thoughtful action. And a concern over crime in the streets did not necessarily reflect inherent fascism; blacks, after all, suffered far more from violence than whites. The notion of running a campaign on the platform of "law and order *with justice*" had a nice theoretical ring.

But the problem, as journalist Samuel Lubell pointed out, could not be so neatly excised. In the 1950s Lubell had written one of the most insightful journalistic books of the decade, *The Future of American Politics,* in which he described the origins of the Roosevelt coalition and its domination of American politics for the next quarter-century. In *The Hidden Crisis in American Politics,* published in early 1970, Lubell detailed the disintegration of that coalition under the pressures of the changes of the 1950s and 1960s.

Lubell saw more clearly than Scammon and Wattenberg the subtleties of the struggle between economics and the social issues among the working class and white-collar lower-middle class. George Wallace, Lubell believed, was the key to understanding just how decisively the balance had shifted toward the new social issues. Unlike Scammon and Wattenberg, however, Lubell had no illusions about the difficulties of peeling off race from these issues.

In 1968, the Wallace vote in the North overwhelmingly reflected the proximity of black Americans to urban whites, whether in their neighborhoods or in their schools. Never random, the Wallace vote was highest in those white enclaves that abutted heavily black districts. Ironically, not poverty, but prosperity, had intensified this racial polarization; the increasing standard of living for black northerners in the 1940s, 1950s, and 1960s had created black neighborhoods on the move, pushing outward toward accessible and affordable housing, often in marginal white communities. Visiting the urban areas that supported Wallace in 1968 was, for Lubell, like "inspecting a stretched-out war front," with each Wallace

29. *Ibid.,* 286–88.

precinct "another outpost marking the borders to which Negro residential movement had pushed." [30]

What was true for neighborhoods in the North was equally true for public schools. The federal courts' shift in focus from legal segregation in the South to insistence upon de facto school integration everywhere created new Wallace voters all over the country. Polling throughout the 1960s showed white northerners to be more comfortable with limited desegregation than their southern counterparts, but once the figures moved toward a 50-percent-black student population, the sectional gap disappeared. Always in the past, said Lubell, the assumption had been that the South would come to resemble the North. "Wallace raised the prospect that the North, as it changes, may become southernized." [31]

Theoretically, it might be possible to separate race from the social issues. Theoretically. In reality, fears of blackness and fears of disorder were the warp and woof of the new social agenda, bound together by the subconscious connection many white Americans made between blackness and criminality, blackness and poverty, blackness and cultural degradation.

Kevin Phillips, the nuts-and-bolts architect of the new Republican majority envisioned by Richard Nixon, made no bones about the importance of race. A youthful graduate of Colgate and Harvard Law School, Phillips was one of the first of that generation of young conservatives who would reshape American politics in the 1980s. His mastery of computerized voter analysis made him an indispensable—but hardly an endeared—part of the Nixon election team. Joe McGinniss, who savagely chronicled the Nixon 1968 television ad campaign, was one of the many who mocked Phillips— "pale and dour" from hours huddled over his computers and charts, hurrying through the halls of Nixon headquarters trailing reams of printouts. Adman Roger Ailes swore that Phillips was stuffed with sawdust; another Nixon aide dubbed him simply "The Computer." [32]

But no one denied his brilliance. Throughout 1968 and much of 1969 he labored away at a book that would have a profound impact on his

30. Samuel Lubell, *The Hidden Crisis in American Politics* (New York: W. W. Norton, 1970), 105.

31. *Ibid.,* 86.

32. McGinniss, *Selling of the President, 1968,* pp. 123–24.

party's future political strategy. *The Emerging Republican Majority* devoted more of its text to political history and tradition than to prescriptions for the future. But with strength and subtlety—and breathless cynicism—the young author offered more than a simple description of what was happening in American politics. Just as Marx foresaw the inevitable triumph of the working class through the inexorable process of dialectical materialism, Phillips believed that the irreversible trends of American politics foreshadowed a shift from a Democratic to a Republican majority. Like Marx, he believed that it was possible to push these processes along.

Race was not the only factor in this transformation of American politics. Like Scammon and Wattenberg, Phillips recognized the significance of the broader cultural issues that had emerged in the mid-1960s. Like them, he emphasized the essential conservatism of first- and second-generation ethnics, and he was perfectly willing to take advantage of the anti-intellectualism that Wallace had brilliantly illuminated in his 1968 campaign. But Phillips bluntly recognized the critical role that white fears would play in guaranteeing the emerging Republican majority. In the traditional Democratic heartland—the urban Midwest—racial assertiveness by blacks within the Democratic Party was driving whites into the Republican Party despite lingering attachments to their earlier New Deal allegiances. And in the South the enfranchisement of black southerners and their movement into the Democratic Party reinforced the conservative revulsion of white southerners and their pell-mell abandonment of the party of their fathers. In a recommendation more suited to Machiavelli, Phillips urged his party to work vigorously to maintain and expand black voting rights in the South, not as a moral issue, but because such a stratagem would hasten the departure of southern whites into the Republican Party.[33]

Understanding what makes politics tick wasn't so difficult, Phillips confided to author Garry Wills in the middle of the 1968 election. Who hates whom: "That is the secret." The trick was to use the emotional issues of culture and race to achieve what Phillips' mentor and boss, John Mitchell, called a "positive polarization" of American politics. (By "positive,"

---

33. Kevin Phillips, *The Emerging Republican Majority* (New Rochelle, N.Y.: Arlington House, 1970), 287.

Mitchell meant that Republicans would end up with more than 50 percent of the voters once the electorate was divided into warring camps.) In the long run, Wallace would be a big help. "People will ease their way into the Republican Party by way of the American Independents. . . . We'll get two-thirds to three-fourths of the Wallace vote in nineteen seventy-two."[34]

Two weeks after Phillips' book came off the press, Harry Dent, by now firmly in control of Nixon's southern command, urged the president to develop a racial policy conservative enough to entice the South from Wallace, but not so radical as to repel the "nominally Democrat white middle-class vote in the swing states of California, Ohio, Illinois, Pennsylvania and New Jersey." In short, said Dent, the Republican Party should "follow Phillips' plan," although—he hastened to add—they should certainly "disavow it publicly."[35]

Over the 1969 Christmas holidays Nixon had his own chance to read the book. He shared Dent's enthusiasm. In his daily meeting with H. R. Haldeman on January 8, 1970, he issued the marching orders: "use [Kevin] Phillips as an analyst—study his strategy—don't think in terms of old-time ethnics, go for Poles, Italians, Irish, must learn to understand Silent Majority . . . don't go for Jews & Blacks."[36]

A month later, Yale law professor Alexander Bickel published an explosive article in the flagship magazine of American liberalism, the *New Republic*. Bickel began with a blunt question: was there any way to prevent whites—particularly middle-class whites—from fleeing integrated school systems outside the South? His answer: an emphatic *no*. Therefore, he argued, since significant school integration was not politically possible in the United States, the nation should seek to improve the educational system as it existed. That is, we should accept de facto segregation as an inevitable creation of intransigent cultural mores.

Richard Nixon had the Bickel article copied and made required reading for all White House staff.[37] In fact, by that time the course of action

34. *Ibid.*, 265, 267.
35. Harry Dent to Richard Nixon, October 13, 1969, in Box 2, Dent Files, RNPM.
36. H. R. Haldeman Notes, January 8, 1970, in Box 41, H. R. Haldeman Papers, RNPM.
37. Alexander M. Bickel, "Where Do We Go From Here?" *New Republic*, February 7, 1970, pp. 20–22.

seemed set: the administration would soft-pedal desegregation as part of a general effort to take advantage of an increasingly conservative electorate, North and South. The new policy prompted the ill-fated attempts to appoint southern conservatives to the United States Supreme Court (the Haynesworth-Carswell debacle) as well as the firing of key HEW civil rights enforcement officials like Leon Panetta. Nixon gently kicked his old friend Robert Finch upstairs to a vague role as "White House adviser." And when Finch's replacement, Elliott Richardson, seemed to show an undue readiness to support federal court busing decrees, the president's memo to John Ehrlichman was unmistakable in intent. "I want you personally to jump Richardson and Justice and tell them to *Knock off this Crap,*" Nixon wrote. "I hold them personally accountable to keep their left-wingers in step with my express policy—Do what the law requires and not *one bit more.*"[38]

The revised policy assured the abandonment of the Family Assistance Plan. Nixon's two most recent biographers disagree over just how committed he was to the program, but the timing of its withdrawal was clearly related to the changing political climate. As the off-year congressional elections approached, Moynihan pleaded with Nixon to throw his support behind the FAP, which had passed the House but was bottled up in the Senate by a coalition of liberal Democrats and conservative Republicans. It was now or never, he warned.

Nixon did nothing. Instead, emphasizing the escalation of violent demonstrations, crime in the streets, and the rise of pornography in America, he hit the road campaigning for fellow Republicans. The Family Assistance Plan died a quiet death in the Congress, although its corpse lingered for another year and a half. In April of 1972, when a cabinet member asked what should be done about the proposed legislation, the president replied with a shrug. "Flush it," he said. "Blame it on the Budget."[39]

The decision to scuttle the Family Assistance Plan marked one of many steps in Nixon's abandonment of his moderate policies on issues of race, welfare, and economics. In the final analysis, the scheme fell victim not to the budget, but to the growing racial tensions in American society, as well

38. Ambrose, *Nixon: The Triumph of a Politician,* 460.
39. Parmet, *Richard Nixon,* 559.

as to the need to maintain the Republican base within the South and among those conservative Democrats outside the region who had first rallied to the cause of George Wallace and would eventually be described as "Reagan Democrats."

By the election of 1972, the turn of the wheel was complete. The president who had promised to "bring us together" unleashed a political campaign that emphasized his commitment to containing welfare costs, his opposition to busing, quotas, and affirmative action (including the repudiation of many of the programs begun by his own administration), and a continued hammering away at the theme that the Democratic Party was out of touch with mainstream values in American society.

But as president, Nixon could move only so far. Wallace would always be on his right flank to criticize his actions as half-hearted and ineffective. And so, as early as the fall of 1969, a secret campaign had been initiated to neutralize George Wallace as a threat to Nixon's—and the Republican Party's—future. Although it would be overshadowed by the Watergate revelations, the struggle was characterized by the same patterns of high-level duplicity, dirty tricks, and back-room deals.

Alabama's governor had been barred from running for reelection in 1966 by the state's constitutional prohibition against consecutive gubernatorial terms. He evaded this restriction by successfully running his wife as a stand-in, but Lurleen Wallace died of cancer in the spring of 1968 and was succeeded by longtime Wallace supporter Albert Brewer. In an uncharacteristic moment of weakness, Wallace promised not to run against Brewer when the former lieutenant governor sought a full term in 1970.

In the fall of 1969, however, Nixon's postmaster general, Winton "Red" Blount, learned that Wallace—deprived of the leverage of the governorship—was having difficulty tapping his usual Alabama business supporters for funds for his 1972 presidential campaign. Blount, a wealthy Montgomery businessman with close ties to Alabama politics, predicted that Wallace would renege on his pledge to Brewer. He was right. In February of 1970, Wallace double-crossed his old friend and announced his candidacy for another term as governor.[40]

40. Author's interview with Winton R. Blount, November 1, 1988; New York *Times*, February 27, 1970.

Unexpectedly, however, a secret White House poll reported the unthinkable: Albert Brewer—soft-spoken, self-effacing, and totally noncharismatic—had a ten-point lead over his challenger. In a lengthy meeting with Haldeman and Nixon, Blount proposed a bold strategy: by funneling badly needed funds to Brewer, he argued, it might be possible to destroy Wallace on his home turf and remove him as a political threat to Republican plans in the South. For two weeks, Nixon uncharacteristically hesitated. Like his southern strategist Harry Dent, he was skeptical of predictions that Brewer could upset George Wallace. Still, in the context of a Nixon reelection campaign kitty bulging with cash collected before the Campaign Reform Act of 1970, there was little concern about the financial cost; the real danger was public disclosure. After several discussions with his loyal friend Attorney General John Mitchell, Nixon authorized the secret plan to derail George Wallace.[41]

The details of that operation offer a striking refutation of claims for the Nixon administration's legendary efficiency and competence. White House aide Larry Higby arranged the first meeting between Nixon attorney Herbert Kalmbach and Brewer aide Robert Ingram and supplied a complex series of secret code words and responses that would have done justice to James Bond ("Are you Mr. Jensen from Baltimore?" "No, I am Mr. Jensen of Detroit."). Unfortunately, such skullduggery apparently works best between the covers of a book. Bob Ingram arrived at New York's Sherry-Netherland Hotel expecting a check for up to $25,000, only to discover a dour Kalmbach clutching a large leather briefcase stuffed with hundred-dollar bills. Ingram didn't have a briefcase; he didn't even have a topcoat or raincoat on that unseasonably warm March morning. When Kalmbach refused to relinquish his expensive leather briefcase, Ingram had no recourse but to bundle the cash into a large manila envelope—in plain sight of two incredulous hotel waiters. He then fled to the safety of his hotel room. Only then did the terrified courier discover that

41. Harry Dent to Richard Nixon, January 19, 1970, February 13, 1970, both Box 4, Dent Files, RNPM; Richard Nixon Memorandum for John Ehrlichman, February 18, 1970, in White House Special Files, Box 83, "Presidential Memos to Ehrlichman, 1970," RNPM; Lawrence N. Higby Deposition, 43–48, in *Democratic National Committee* v. *James McCord,* DNC Papers, United States Archives, Washington, D.C.

he had been walking down Fifth Avenue with *one thousand* hundred-dollar bills.[42]

When the two Alabamians continued to run neck and neck, President Nixon authorized another $300,000 in cash, but his premonition had been right. Despite a strong early lead and a near victory in the first runoff in May, the soft-spoken Brewer was out of his league. His opponent unleashed one of the most racist campaigns in modern southern political history. Wallace derided his former legislative floor leader as a "sissy britches" politician who "used to stand on this platform behind me and my wife. . . , who rode her skirttails to power [and now has] joined together with black militants to defeat me." In a barrage of radio, television, and newspaper ads, Wallace pleaded with white voters to "save Alabama as you know Alabama" and charged that, should Brewer win, the state would be ruled by a "spotted alliance" of blacks and "sissy britches from Harvard who spend most of their time in a country club drinking tea with their finger stuck up." On one occasion, unaware that television cameras were recording his remarks, Wallace put the issue bluntly to a group of Gadsden factory workers: "300,000 nigger votes is mighty hard to overcome."[43]

Meanwhile, a trusted aide coordinated a scurrilous underground campaign. Mysteriously funded "independent" Committees for Wallace ran newspaper ads showing a blond little girl sitting on a beach surrounded by seven grinning black adolescent boys. The caption warned: "This Could Be Alabama Four Years From Now." Radio spots depicted the dramatic sounds of a police siren, two cars pulling to the side of the road, and then the ominous narration: "Suppose your wife is driving home at 11 o'clock at night. She is stopped by a highway patrolman. He turns out to be black. Think about it. . . . Elect George Wallace." Contrived photographs showed Brewer allegedly accepting an endorsement from Black Muslim Elijah Muhammad and fighter Cassius Clay/Muhammad Ali; there was even one purporting to show Brewer's daughter pregnant by a secret black lover.[44]

42. Author's interview with Robert Ingram, July 15, 1988; Bob Ingram, *That's the Way I Saw It* (Montgomery, Ala.: Privately printed, 1986), 16–22.

43. Birmingham *Post-Herald*, April 30, 1970; Montgomery *Advertiser*, April 30, 1970; New York *Times*, June 7, 1940; *Newsweek*, June 15, 1970.

44. Birmingham *News*, April 21, 1970; Birmingham *Post-Herald*, April 21, April 30, 1970.

In the June 2 runoff, Wallace charged back from a 10,000-vote deficit in the first primary to defeat Albert Brewer decisively and to place himself squarely, once again, in the running for 1972.

Publicly, Nixon and his aides insisted that the Alabamian's openly racist campaign had made him damaged goods; privately, the president remained preoccuppied by Wallace's resourceful comeback. On July 19, Nixon wrote in firm, underlined letters on his ever-present yellow pad: "*Need to handle Wallace.*" Later that month, Attorney General Mitchell named a special assistant to head up a massive Internal Revenue Service investigation under the code name "The Alabama Project."

Richard Nixon repeatedly groused that he did not invent the practice of using the nation's tax system to harass political enemies. And he was right. During the Roosevelt and Kennedy administrations in particular, representatives of the executive branch abused the tax system by triggering politically motivated audits. But Nixon and his staff raised the abuse of the IRS to an art form. In July of 1969, White House assistant Tom Huston (of later "Plumber's" fame) pressured the IRS into forming a "Special Services Staff" to target and investigate "leftist" political individuals and organizations; by 1970 the enemies list had been broadened well beyond the original scope of Huston's mandate.

Even before the Wallace-Brewer contest, H. R. Haldeman had learned that the IRS had an ongoing investigation of political corruption in Alabama. He leaked a summary of the findings to columnist Jack Anderson two weeks before the first primary.[45] In the absence of concrete evidence, Wallace was able to brush aside the Anderson column as a transparent attempt by the Nixon administration to play politics; it seems to have done him little damage in the 1970 campaign.

What had been a relatively low-key investigation moved into high gear in late summer, however, as more than sixty IRS agents and Justice Department representatives pored over the records of Alabama agencies and state contractors. In April of 1971, federal prosecuting attorneys began presenting the results of their two-year probe to a Montgomery grand jury.

45. Clark Mollenhoff, "Statement of Information and Supporting Evidence," Watergate Hearings, Committee on the Judiciary, pp. 33–42; Clark R. Mollenhoff, *Game Plan for Disaster: An Ombudsman's Report on the Nixon Years* (New York, W. W. Norton, 1976), 108–17.

Despite the supposed confidentiality of the proceedings, knowledgeable local reporters learned that although George Wallace would not be named, prosecutors planned to indict his brother Gerald and at least a dozen major Wallace business supporters who had made millions off their contracts with the state government.[46]

The events of the next thirty days are among the most disputed in the twisted relationship of Richard Nixon and George Wallace.

These facts are not in question:

On April 30, without explanation, the federal prosecuting attorney in the case suddenly announced a temporary recess in the presentation of witnesses to the grand jury.

Two weeks later, on a speaking tour of the Southeast, Nixon invited Wallace to join him aboard the presidential helicopter flying from Mobile to Birmingham.

On May 29, columnist Rowland Evans, known for his sources in the Nixon White House, reported that Postmaster General Blount was back in Alabama for a series of secret meetings with Wallace. According to sources in the postmaster general's office, Wallace told Blount that they had a common interest in keeping a liberal Democrat out of the White House.

The grand jury finally reconvened in early September, but instead of indicting Gerald Wallace and close supporters of the governor, it returned indictments against only a handful of Alabama business and political leaders, all but one of whom had broken with Wallace between 1968 and 1971.

On January 12, 1972, the Justice Department announced that it was dropping its investigation of Gerald Wallace and dismissing the grand jury.

Twenty-four hours later, George Wallace announced in a Montgomery press conference that he was a candidate for president of the United States—but would run in the Democratic primaries, not as a third-party candidate.

---

46. Birmingham *News,* April 10, 11, 18, 30, 1971. Shortly after the June 1970 runoff, John Mitchell had confided to Charles Colson that Wallace was in a "peck of trouble." He seemed confident that the IRS investigation would immobilize Wallace. "I remember thinking to myself, 'Boy that's good news,'" Colson later recalled, "'because that'll get him out of the way for 1972.'" Charles W. Colson interview, June 15, 1988, RNPM.

Was a deal made in 1971, an agreement to trade tax fraud charges for Wallace's promise to run in the Democratic primaries? The question is not easily answered, since President Nixon tenaciously—and success-fully—resisted the release of many of his files that might shed light on the issue. Nor is it certain that the Nixon papers would contain a "smoking gun." Although Richard Nixon's penchant for recording his own conver-sations helped to lead to his downfall, members of his administration who were engaged in potentially embarrassing activities tried to follow the ad-vice Louisiana's Earl Long had given to his underlings: "Don't write any-thing you can phone. Don't phone anything you can talk face to face. Don't talk anything you can smile. Don't smile anything you can wink. Don't wink anything you can nod." And the key players who may have talked, smiled, winked, or nodded are either dead, as in the case of John Mitchell and Gerald Wallace, or they have been remarkably forgetful, as in the case of George Wallace, former postmaster general Blount, and Richard Kleindienst, John Mitchell's successor. (Like his predecessor, Kleindienst micromanaged the Justice Department's investigation of cor-ruption in Alabama and cleared all important prosecutorial decisions with the White House.)

Whether or not an explicit agreement was made, Wallace's decision to abandon his third-party effort was an act of extraordinary importance for the Nixon reelection campaign strategists. No longer would they have to worry about responding to Wallace; he was the Democrats' problem. Should he win the nomination—an extremely unlikely prospect—Nixon could move just to his left and swamp him in the general election. More likely, one White House aide predicted, Wallace would move through the Democratic primaries like a pyromaniac in the middle of a fireworks fac-tory, leaving the party in shambles.[47]

And indeed, the Wallace candidacy was a major factor in the collapse of the Democrats in 1972. In the Florida primary, Wallace faced a well-financed field of candidates—Birch Bayh, Hubert Humphrey, George McGovern, Henry Jackson, Edmund Muskie, John Lindsay, Shirley Chisholm, Vance Hartke, Wilbur Mills, and Sam Yorty. The Alabama

---

47. As Nixon told biographer Herbert Parmet, he never had any concern about Mc-Govern: "My concern was about Wallace." Parmet, *Richard Nixon,* 627.

governor took 42 percent of the votes; no one else came close. In Pennsylvania and Indiana, he narrowly lost to Hubert Humphrey, who had the frenzied support of organized labor and outspent him eight to one. By mid-May, Wallace had polled a total of 3.3 million votes to 2.5 million for Humphrey and 2.1 million for McGovern. Through April and early May, White House aides Charles Colson, Harry Dent, and Pat Buchanan passed along private polls and off-the-record suggestions as the rogue Democrat tore the party apart with savage attacks on antiwar demonstrators and busing and "forced integration." Branching out from the traditional politics of racism, Wallace gave shape and focus to a whole range of social issues, from abortion to banned Bible readings to crime in the streets—the social issues that would come to dominate the rhetoric of American politics.

And then, on May 15, came the macabre replay of a scene Americans witnessed repeatedly in the 1960s: a psychopathic loner—Arthur Bremer—a crowd, the muted sound of a small handgun, and then screams and confusion. Unlike Medgar Evers, John and Robert Kennedy, and Martin Luther King, George Wallace would survive, but his spinal cord was partially severed. Never again would he charge across the stage with that wild rhetoric that brought cheering supporters to their feet and left opponents enraged. In the primaries in Tennessee, North Carolina, Maryland, and Michigan—some of them held the day after Arthur Bremer gunned him down in a Maryland shopping center—Wallace swept the field. But the badly injured candidate was forced to withdraw from the race.[48]

48. His most stunning victory came in Michigan, where he won 51 percent of the vote to George McGovern's 27 percent and Humphrey's 16 percent. The Michigan result, I might add, can be explained primarily in terms of that spring's Richmond, Virginia, federal court decision (later overturned) calling for the consolidation of inner-school districts with those of suburban communities. In the Michigan primary, Wallace drew as well in the white-collar Republican suburban districts as in his expected white blue-collar strongholds. New York *Times,* May 14, 1972, p. 39; Detroit *News,* May 17, 1972. There are no studies of the 1972 presidential campaign comparable to the outstanding book by English journalists Lewis Chester, Godfrey Hodgson, and Bruce Page, *An American Melodrama: The Presidential Campaign of 1968* (New York: Viking Press, 1969). Wallace's papers in the Alabama Department of Archives and History are useful, but incomplete for the campaign. I have relied

Franklin Roosevelt survived paralysis and went on to become president. Wallace's precipitous political collapse is a reminder of the essentially sexual nature of his appeal. His 1976 run for the presidency was a pathetic last hurrah. Later that same year he became embroiled in a public scandal with his second wife over fears that she sought sexual favors elsewhere. Alabama newspapers reported—with all the discretion one would expect—the sordid details of wiretapping, secret trysts, and pathetically obscene late night telephone calls from Wallace to his old lovers. Although he managed to squeak through with one last gubernatorial victory in 1982, his name was as likely to provoke a smirk as a salute by the end of his career.

George Wallace was finished, and so, for the time being, was the Democratic Party, which went down to devastating defeat in November of 1972. Richard Nixon had understood Wallace's political role; the 1972 campaign marked a critical realignment in American politics. Nixon had successfully pulled a substantial number of traditionally Democratic ethnic and blue-collar workers into the Grand Old Party. And, what was more important, he had brought most of the southern Wallace voters into the Republican column.

The "gut" issues of the future would be crime, busing, drugs, welfare, inflation. All of these, said Nixon with some satisfaction, were "issues the Democrats [Wallace excepted] hate." [49] And the growing Republican dominance in the South was the single most important outcome of the election of 1972. With Wallace finally out of the picture, it would be possible for the Republican Party to build a "New American Majority" on the solid foundation of the conservative South. [50]

---

upon a wide variety of secondary and primary materials ranging from newspaper coverage (the New York *Times*, the Washington *Post*, the Los Angeles *Times*, the Birmingham *News*, and the Montgomery *Advertiser*) to the Haldeman political files in the Nixon Presidential Archives, Alexandria, Va.

49. Richard Nixon to John Ehrlichman, April 8, 1972, in Box 163, Haldeman Files, RNPM. See also Nixon to Ehrlichman, May 17, 1972, *ibid.*

50. As Nixon said in the Haldeman diaries (released in early 1994), elitists might "look down their noses" at southerners, but in fact southerners were "Americans to the core," a people who had never been "poisoned by the elite universities and the media," so that they retained their "patriotism," "strong moral and spiritual values," and "anti-permissiveness."

The 1972 GOP campaign set the framework for the political struggles of the next two decades by convincing voters, particularly Wallace voters, that they faced the choice of Nixon, who seemed to favor the rich, or McGovern—who apparently supported shiftless poor blacks, left-wing protesters, and sexual degenerates. They did not hesitate in their choice. And that, in fact, was the great legacy of the election of 1972: the successful identification of the Republican Party with the values of an increasingly conservative America. Richard Nixon promised law and order at home and a foreign policy based upon a strong military defense. In contrast, the message of McGovern's Democrats could be summed up in the twin phrases of Nixon speechwriter Pat Buchanan: "weakness abroad, permissiveness at home." Just as Scammon and Wattenberg had predicted, the Democratic Party was identified overwhelmingly with the interests of black Americans in an increasingly polarized America.

The Watergate scandal sent Nixon into exile and made it possible for a soft-spoken Georgia ex-governor to claim the White House in 1976, but the Carter victory did little to alter the fundamental realities of American politics. In the struggle to identify the most appealing and powerful symbols, Richard Nixon and the leaders of the Republican Party had placed themselves on the crest of a rising wave of conservatism.

These quotations are from the October 14, 1972, entry in the CD-ROM edition of Robert Haldeman's *The Haldeman Diaries,* released in 1994 by the Sony Corporation's Imagesoft Division. G. P. Putnam's Sons published an abbreviated version the same year as *The Haldeman Diaries: Inside the Nixon White House,* but many of the most important references to Wallace are to be found only in the unedited CD-ROM edition.

3 | THE POLITICS OF SYMBOLS

Ronald Reagan captured the White House on the strength of his charismatic personality and a broad-based disillusionment with the administration of Jimmy Carter. The Californian's views on foreign policy leapfrogged past Nixon back to Barry Goldwater. In his successful 1980 campaign he called for a massive military build-up that would assure American dominance—rather than parity—vis-à-vis the Soviet Union, and for a tough-minded foreign policy that deemphasized Carter's fuzzy notions of "human rights." And he couched the complex issues of third-world conflicts in the luridly fluorescent shades of the Cold War—*i.e.,* pro-American authoritarian regimes were good; anti-American totalitarian regimes were bad.

Reagan's domestic policies also had their roots in Goldwater Republicanism but were far more convoluted. On issues of race, Reagan compiled an abysmal record in his sixteen years as governor of California and president of the United States. In California he proposed a repeal of the Rumford Act, which prohibited an owner from offering property for sale or rent and then withdrawing it for racial or religious reasons. When a group of black legislators met with him to protest, he borrowed a line straight out of George Wallace's campaign speeches of 1968 and insisted his opposition to the measure had nothing to do with race discrimination. "You wouldn't want to sell your house to a red-headed Kiwanian if you didn't want to, would you?" he asked the nonplussed delegation. Unfortunately, we do not have a record of their response. Reagan opposed the

Civil Rights Act of 1964, and he vehemently attacked the landmark Voting Rights Act of 1965 as a measure "humiliating" to southerners—a description that, as Julian Bond dryly observed, said a great deal about whom Governor Reagan considered a southerner. It is fair to suggest—in an inversion of Will Rogers' comment—that the Californian never met a civil rights bill he liked, an attitude that continued to mark his two terms as president.[1]

Although Reagan appointed a number of moderate Republicans in his first administration, he signaled his approach on civil rights with the decision to name William Bradford Reynolds as assistant attorney general for civil rights. Reynolds, a Yale-educated lawyer, brought to his position a zealous hostility to the nation's civil rights leadership and—like most of Reagan's top appointees—a finely tuned sensitivity to the political implications of his decisions. Much of the Reynolds program continued those conservative policies pioneered by Richard Nixon in the last three years of his administration: reductions in the enforcement budget of the Civil Rights Division of the Justice Department, unwavering opposition to busing for school integration, and a vigorous hostility to any measure that Reynolds and his boss, Ed Meese, concluded smacked of discrimination against white men. Above all, Reynolds represented the widespread belief in the Reagan administration that it was impermissible to use policies to promote groups that might have suffered past discrimination—*i.e.,* blacks—against the interests of individuals in the present—*i.e.,* whites.[2]

Occasionally Reynolds stepped over the boundaries of the new conservative consensus. Beginning in the Carter administration and continuing through the 1970s, the Justice Department had consistently held that private schools practicing racial discrimination would not be granted tax-exempt status, a measure particularly galling to the more than one hundred, mostly ultra-right-wing, religious schools denied such status. In late 1981, Representative Trent Lott of Mississippi wrote to Reagan, complaining that these tax policies discriminated against many of the

1. Ronnie Dugger, *On Reagan: The Man and His Presidency* (New York: McGraw-Hill, 1983), 198.
2. Reynolds' record as assistant attorney general for civil rights was laid out during his confirmation hearing when Reagan unsuccessfully attempted to name him as associate attorney general, the number-two position in the Justice Department. New York *Times,* June 19, 23, 28, 30, 1985.

president's most loyal supporters. Lott asked that Reagan intervene and grant exemptions to the law. In the margin of Lott's letter, the president noted: "I think we should."[3] Without public hearings, on January 8, 1982, William Bradford Reynolds joined Bob Jones University and the Goldsboro, North Carolina, Christian Schools in a brief in federal court to strike down the bar on granting tax-exempt status.

Within a week, complaints deluged the Reagan administration. The usually even-tempered New York *Times* labeled the turnabout a "racist policy" that promoted "tax-exempt hate." When the president defended his action and claimed there was "no basis in the law" for denying tax-exempt status to segregated institutions, more than 100 of the 175 lawyers in the Civil Rights Division signed a petition arguing that such an exemption was a clear violation of the law. (A Justice Department spokesman for Reynolds announced to the press that the attorneys were "welcome to leave." More than 20 did so.) The following year, the United States Supreme Court brushed aside the briefs filed by Reynolds, Bob Jones University, and the Goldsboro Christian Schools in an 8–1 decision declaring that IRS policy against such exemptions was "wholly consistent with what Congress, the executive and the courts have repeatedly declared."[4]

In the short run, the unsuccessful effort of the Meese Justice Department to support the racist policies of religious conservatives embarrassed the Reagan administration, but in the long run the move provided a political boost. Conservative white evangelicals had begun their exodus to the Republican Party in the 1960s and 1970s, but the threat to their tax-exempt status did much to motivate the religious right, and Reagan's support for their cause increased their tilt toward Republican conservatism in the years that followed.[5]

3. Laurence I. Barrett, *Gambling with History: Ronald Reagan in the White House* (Garden City, N.Y.: Doubleday, 1963), 426.

4. Although his account is unremittingly hostile to Reynolds, journalist Ronnie Dugger gives the best summary of these issues in the early stages of the Reagan administration in *On Reagan,* 195–219. (The title of the relevant chapter aptly captures Dugger's point of view: "All These Beautiful White People.") Thomas and Mary Edsall describe the angry response of evangelicals in *Chain Reaction: The Impact of Race, Rights, and Taxes on American Politics* (New York: W. W. Norton, 1991), 131–33.

5. See Dan Balz and Ronald Browstein, *Storming the Gates: Protest Politics and the Republican Revival* (Boston: Little, Brown & Co., 1996).

Reagan again appeared to suffer a setback when the Voting Rights Act came up for renewal in 1982. He first sought to eviscerate the legislation; only when he realized that there remained widespread bipartisan support for renewal did he endorse the bill. But temporary embarrassment did not translate into long-term political damage. Driven by both ideology and the conviction it was swimming with the tide of public opinion, the Civil Rights Division under Reynolds kept up a barrage of briefs attacking a whole range of affirmative action programs, many of which had been adopted by wide bipartisan agreement. Bluntly, the assistant attorney general repeated his view that government had no business trying to correct historic patterns of discrimination; his agency functioned only to protect individuals from specific acts of discrimination.

In dealing with the issues of economic rights and educational opportunities for blacks, Reynolds was inflexible: his task was to ensure equality of opportunity for individuals, not equality of results for groups. When it came to voting rights, however, he reversed himself. In case after case through the early 1980s, he sought to maximize the effects of the black vote on political representation by supporting single-member, rather than at-large, electoral districts and by redrawing districts to guarantee the election of black officials. Kevin Phillips' *Emerging Republican Majority* had laid out the rationale for this ideological inconsistency. As blacks were drained from biracial districts, Phillips predicted, conservative Republicans would defeat white Democratic moderates. And the Democratic gains made by the election of a handful of blacks would be offset by the broad-scale defection of whites to the Republican Party.[6]

In the long run, the ideological thrust of Reagan's judicial appointments probably had a far greater impact than the specific racial policies of his Justice Department. Guided by a task force operating out of the newly created Office of Legal Policy, Republican ideologues compiled extensive dossiers on each potential appointment and—in a break from tradition—brought the candidates to Washington for detailed interviews to make certain that (as one Justice Department aide put it) "maverick moderates" did not make it to the bench. During his eight years in office,

6. Kevin Phillips, *The Emerging Republican Majority* (New Rochelle, N.Y.: Arlington House, 1970), 287.

Ronald Reagan reshaped the federal judiciary to a degree matched only by Franklin Roosevelt. He named 5 Supreme Court justices, 78 appeals court judges, and 290 district court judges—more than half of the federal judiciary. Collectively, his appointees were economically conservative, youthful, white, male, and uniformly hostile to affirmative action policies.[7]

More critical than the specific judicial policies of the Reagan administration, however, was the economic impact of the sweeping changes wrought in tax policy and federal expenditures.

The Reagan economic program reflected traditional Republican views: a generalized animosity to the welfare state, a preference for lower taxes, and a boundless faith in the efficacy of laissez-faire economics. Reagan's most insightful biographer, Garry Wills, saw his subject's childlike faith in capitalism in theological terms. St. Augustine, the classic expositor of the notion of Original Sin, spoke of what he called the inevitable sequences of disaster that flowed from man's attempt to be free of the consequences of Adam's fall—free, as we would put it in more secular terms, of history.

Reagan, in contrast, was part and parcel of the American ethos that has historically resisted such pessimistic angst. America was a new land, a nation set upon a hill without the burdensome memories of a failed past. It was no accident, said Wills, that Reagan so successfully dismissed the hapless Jimmy Carter. Carter may not have read St. Augustine, but he was a disciple of Reinhold Niebuhr, who believed that mindless optimism was the ultimate form of hubris. Carter's outlook was shaped by the echoes of St. Augustine's warnings; thus, the Georgia-born Baptist talked of limits and self-denial, of aggression and pain. At its heart, the science of governing was a willingness to engage in an endless struggle to control man's sinful nature, a struggle with no fade-out on a happy ending, only the satisfaction of holding back the darkness.

If the doctrine of the Fall suggested that men and women were inevitably entangled in each other's errors, Ronald Reagan lived by the countermyth of the Market: private vices became public good through the ministrations of Adam Smith's invisible hand. "Individual greeds add up to general gain," wrote Garry Wills, so long as the nation is spared the

7. Sheldon Goldman, "Reagan's Judicial Legacy: Completing the Puzzle and Summing Up," *Judicature,* April–May, 1989.

stifling hand of government. "The Market thus produces a happy outcome from endless miseries." [8]

If Reagan's laissez-faire views seem thoroughly conventional, he did make one dubious contribution to the field of public economics. The American economy had stalled through the 1970s because of a troublesome combination of inflation and low economic growth—"stagflation," Carter's opponents called it. Traditional economists bickered back and forth over causes and prescriptions for change. The one thing they agreed upon, however, was that the cure would be painful. That was not a message the ever-upbeat Reagan found appealing. He moved quickly to embrace an alternative that had begun to emerge in the 1970s: supply-side economics.

The doctrine of supply-side economics began with the truism that taxation can be so excessive as to destroy the economy. From that unassailable observation, several amateur conservative journalists and business boosters, led by a bizarre but persuasive academic showman named Arthur Laffer, constructed a chain of assumptions that went something like this: an end to "red tape" and government intervention in the economy, coupled with massive reductions in federal taxes, would promote savings; these savings in turn would create new capital; new capital would lead to new investment, which (along with accelerated depreciation schedules and an eased regulatory climate) would result in cheaper production; lower production costs would make possible lower prices; lower prices would curb inflation and simultaneously boost demand, resulting in an expanded, but noninflationary, economy. As the final stage of this economic transformation, tax revenues would rise to such an extent that they would compensate for those lost in the original tax cut.

At first glance, supply-side economics seemed to be little more than a variation on Keynesian economics, which emphasizes the importance of taxation and monetary policies in expanding and contracting demand within the economic system to smooth out the inevitable business cycles of boom and bust. But there were critical differences. First, Lord Keynes had argued that tax relief should be concentrated on the lower end of the

8. Garry Wills, *Reagan's America: Innocents at Home* (New York: Doubleday, 1987), 384.

economic spectrum, in the belief that low- and moderate-income workers would quickly boost the economy by spending their additional income. Second, cuts were to be used during periods of economic slowdown, but taxes had to be restored when the economy seemed to be accelerating. (This point was one that many of Keynes's political disciples were understandably reluctant to embrace.)

Although they always talked in terms of a general tax decrease, advocates of supply-side economics made no effort to conceal their belief that their most important goal was the reduction of tax rates on the wealthy. Implicit in this analysis was the assumption that low- and lower-middle-income workers tended to dissipate their income in incremental consumer purchases rather than investing in capital-creating equities that would ignite the engine of growth. And the dramatic growth of a supply-side economy would make countercyclical tax increases unnecessary.

Laffer's theories had been popularized through the writings of a number of followers, notably Jude Wanniski, an editorial writer for the *Wall Street Journal.* Wanniski's best-selling 1978 book, *The Way the World Works: How Economies Fail—and Succeed,* became something of a Bible to younger Republican conservatives. Only someone inspired by a Damascus-like vision could have written *The Way the World Works.* Wanniski moved briskly from observations on industrial policies in Europe to the lessons of ancient Rome, forward again through a survey of the shambles of the modern African nation-states, then on to ruminations on the great failure of ancient Chinese civilization (they didn't believe in free trade), and finally to the lessons to be learned from the economic vibrancy of emerging East Asian economies. Throughout his odyssey, he hammered away at the central arguments that came to dominate neoconservative thought. Liberal economic theory—particularly the tired Keynesian model of the postdepression modern world—not only doomed industrial economies to stagnation but was ultimately authoritarian and antidemocratic because it gave undue power to faceless bureaucrats and liberal ideologues who did not trust the people to know their own best self-interests.[9] Only

9. Jude Wanniski: *The Way the World Works: How Economies Fail—and Succeed* (New York: Basic Books, 1978).

with the destruction of the liberal welfare state and the substitution of the free and untrammeled workings of the marketplace could true democracy flourish. For the helping hand of a benevolent government, conservatives would substitute individual initiative and "self-empowerment."

No one was more enthusiastic about Wanniski's ideas than Republican congressman Jack Kemp. He introduced a proposal in Congress for dramatically reducing the upper limits on the progressive income tax and tirelessly promoted Wanniski's argument that cutting taxes on the wealthy would unleash enough growth to compensate for any lost federal revenue. Reagan's 1980 campaign manager, John Sears, assigned Kemp the task of converting his boss. It was not a hard sell. The new president found supply-side economics appealing because it so perfectly matched both his optimistic, upbeat personality and his hostility to big government and high taxes. And it seemed a politician's dream: a free lunch—at least until the bills came due in the next generation.

If it was a free lunch for the politicians who proposed it, Reaganomics/ supply-side economics proved devastating to low-income Americans, particularly the black poor. Few undertakings are as fraught with statistical peril as an attempt to isolate the effect of Reaganomics on the declining economic condition of low-income Americans in general—and black Americans specifically—during the 1980s. Any analysis must be set against the backdrop of a number of factors only indirectly related to government policy: stagnating levels of economic productivity, the internationalization of trade, the increased immigration of unskilled labor, the decline of trade unions, and the technological disruption of the labor market. At the same time, the continuing rise of one-parent households, particularly in the nation's black community, exacerbated other negative economic forces.

Still, some facts are irrefutable. Despite all the talk of tax cuts, Reagan's policy brought significant benefits to a minority of the population. The bottom 50 percent actually saw significant tax increases as social security and excise levies more than offset marginal declines in the income tax rates. Those between the 50th and 90th percentile experienced relatively little change. In contrast, the closer to the top of the pyramid, the greater the reduction in the effective federal tax rates. The top 10 percent enjoyed a 5-percent cut in taxes; the top 1 percent, a 15-percent cut.

Not surprisingly, the nation's richest 5 percent saw a dramatic increase in income during the 1980s. A study completed in 1992 by the Congressional Budget Office showed that the top 1 percent of the population obtained a 60-percent increase in its income *after taxes* during the decade. In contrast, middle income levels remained stagnant, while the bottom fifth of America's wage earners saw their earnings go *down* 10 percent.[10] At the same time, the freezing—and in many cases the actual reduction in real dollars—of federal programs targeted for the poor accentuated this shift in wealth from the bottom upward.

While all lower-income Americans suffered during the 1980s, blacks as a group were hit hardest by the combination of structural changes in the economy. The adoption of low-income tax credits only partially offset the more significant negative impact of changes in the tax structure and reductions in levels of federal welfare. As Thomas and Mary Edsall concluded in their book *Chain Reaction,* middle-to-upper-income African Americans had a steady if unspectacular improvement in their earnings throughout the 1970s and 1980s. But the bottom 10 percent—already desperately poor—experienced an 18-percent decline in family income between 1979 and 1987, a decline which meant that the average black family in that group struggled to survive on less than $98 a week. And that figure included all earned income, direct welfare, housing assistance, food stamps, and the total actual estimated value of medical assistance. By 1990, blacks in the bottom 20 percent of the nation's population were poorer in relation to whites than at any time since the 1950s.[11]

Because my subject is the interrelationship of race and presidential politics since the 1960s, it may seem odd to spend so much time talking about

10. New York *Times,* March 5, 1992. As early as 1987, Frank Levy documented with meticulous detail the general impact of the Reagan tax cuts in his study *Dollars and Dreams: The Changing American Income Distribution* (New York: Russell Sage Foundation, 1987), development described in journalistic prose by Kevin Phillips' more polemical *The Politics of Rich and Poor: Wealth and the American Electorate in the Reagan Aftermath* (New York: Random House, 1990).

11. See, for example, the Edsalls' chapter "White Suburbs and a Divided Black Community" in their book *Chain Reaction.* The disparate impact of the 1960–1990 period on the black middle class and the black poor is a major conclusion of Hugh Davis Graham in his study *The Civil Rights Era: Origins and Development of National Policy* (New York: Oxford University Press, 1990).

the broader context of Reaganomics. But it was in that arena that the politics of race were played out for nearly eight years. And Reagan, with his mastery of the politics of symbolism, managed to shape federal policies far more conservative than those of the Nixon or Bush administration while avoiding many of the public-relations problems that both his predecessors and his successors would have in dealing with the Tar Baby of American racial politics.

Occasionally in the years before his election as president, the former actor had veered over the line of good taste on racial issues. At a 1965 luncheon with Massachusetts attorney general Edward Brooke, he joked that some lunches were better than others. In some of those African nations, for example, said Reagan, "when they have a man for lunch, they really have him for lunch." Brooke, the Republican Party's most visible black political figure in the 1960s and 1970s, was not amused. Equally embarrassing was a slip of the tongue at a 1976 Florida rally when Reagan was trying to wrest the Republican nomination from Gerald Ford. Working people, Reagan told a crowd of Fort Lauderdale whites, were rightly outraged when they waited in grocery lines while a "strapping young buck" ahead of them bought T-bone steaks with food stamps. After a hasty conference with campaign manager John Sears, the candidate reformulated his complaint. The next day at Fort Walton Beach, "some young fellow" was buying the steaks.[12]

Such mishaps were uncharacteristic and inconsistent with Reagan's emphasis on an upbeat and positive message. In his years in the California governorship and in his three presidential campaigns, Reagan showed that he could use coded language with the best of them, lambasting welfare queens, busing, and affirmative action as the need arose. But even when he lashed out against the "liberals," he always sounded like an avuncular uncle reluctantly scolding because he saw no alternative.[13]

Essentially a sunny personality, Ronald Reagan preferred inspirational anecdotes that ended on an "up" note; when asked to talk about segre-

12. Dugger, *On Reagan*, 201.
13. Despite Reagan's identification with the use of the "welfare queen" stories, these were actually more characteristic of his 1976 primary campaign against Ford than of his 1980 and 1984 presidential campaigns. New York *Times*, February 15, 1976; Washington *Post*, January 28, 1976.

gation or race relations, he had an endless number of such uplifting stories. One of his favorites was of how segregation ended in the armed forces. According to Reagan, the shift in policy stemmed from the bravery of a black kitchen worker on board a navy ship docked at Pearl Harbor in December of 1941. When the black sailor heard the sound of the Japanese attack, he "cradled a machine gun in his arms . . . and stood on the end of a pier blazing away at Japanese airplanes that were coming down and strafing him." Because of his bravery and the heroism of other black soldiers and sailors, concluded the president, Generals MacArthur and Eisenhower ended segregation in the armed forces. The story itself was factual nonsense, a combination of scenes from the John Garfield movie *Air Force* (1943) and an army propaganda film produced for the folks back home. And it would have come as news to black servicemen of the 1940s that segregation had ended in World War II; not until 1948 did Harry Truman order an end to military segregation, and Jim Crow units remained in existence until well into the Korean War.[14]

And despite his best efforts, Reagan the political pro seemed to have a tin ear when it came to addressing black audiences. When he made a rare appearance before a nonwhite audience at the 1981 NAACP national convention, he ended his speech by recounting the story of Garfield Langhorn, a black soldier who received the Medal of Honor posthumously for throwing himself on a live grenade in order to save several of his fellow soldiers in Vietnam. According to Reagan, who ended the story with a catch in his voice, Langhorn's last words were: "You have to care." Actually, Langhorn never regained consciousness, and in any case, black listeners questioned the relevance of the president's message.[15]

But the anecdote reflected the quintessential Reagan: intent on sifting from grubby facts and tiresome details a larger and more congenial truth. His handlers initially lived in a constant state of terror that he would unload another outlandish misstatement. They often felt their main function was to shepherd Reagan away from the symbolically appealing but factually inaccurate stories he loved so well. Halfway through his first term, two New York journalists compiled a best-selling paperback entitled

14. Wills, *Reagan's America,* 165.
15. Denver *Post,* June 30, 1981.

There He Goes Again: Ronald Reagan's Reign of Error.[16] Sometimes hilarious, often sobering, the book compiled more than four hundred factual errors Reagan had breezily uttered in his years in public life. But Mark Green and Gail MacColl did not, in the vernacular, "get it." Long before the former movie star's 1984 reelection campaign, the men who surrounded Ronald Reagan realized that their fears were groundless. Adman Roger Ailes explained: "I call it the magic bullet, because if your audience likes you [as in the case of Reagan], they'll forgive just about everything else you do wrong. If they don't like you, you can hit every rule right on target and it doesn't matter."[17] The president's geniality and his apparent sincerity would usually override any misgivings about questions of fact.

Ronald Reagan proved to be the president that only central casting could have created, for he brought hope and optimism to a badly shaken nation. During the turbulent sixties, the signposts of a generation seemed to have been swept away in a revolution made all the more menacing by the electronic visions of turmoil and upheaval that flashed across America's living rooms each evening. The impact on race relations was particularly profound. Most whites living in working-class communities, said essayist Pete Hamill, saw blacks only as "militants with Afros and shades, or crushed people on welfare." According to the repeated video message, most blacks were "threatening to burn down America or asking for help or receiving welfare or committing crime."[18]

Television had played a powerful role in the acceleration of the civil rights movement in the first half of the 1960s; it furnished an equal impetus to the counterrevolution of the late 1960s and early 1970s. Marshall Frady, Wallace's first biographer, saw it when he interviewed voters in the white working-class precincts of Gary, Indiana, after the 1968 election. For much of the decade, they had watched the stories of rising crime and racial tensions, the burning of great American cities, and the emergence of a black leadership demanding—not asking—for a place at the table of

16. Mark Green and Gail MacColl, *There He Goes Again: Ronald Reagan's Reign of Error* (New York: Pantheon Books, 1983).

17. Roger Ailes with Jon Kraushar, *You Are the Message: Secrets of the Master Communicators* (Homewood, Ill.: Dow Jones–Irwin, 1988), 69.

18. Pete Hamill, "The Revolt of the White Lower-Middle Class," *New York,* April 14, 1969, p. 28.

American democracy. Their community, their neighborhood, might be relatively calm, wrote Frady, but through the "immediacy of television," they felt "menaced by confrontations and figures remote from their existences, which in another time would have remained quite abstract to them."[19]

The chaos and disorder reflected on their flickering television screens reminded working-class and lower-middle-class families that the vaunted American virtues of mobility and choice—*control*—belonged to another world. While young executives and well-educated Americans on the way up might welcome risk and opportunity, the average working-class and lower-income white-collar worker found it difficult to imagine major change for the better. He (or she) had no problem envisioning change for the worse. And yet, said essayist Peter Schrag, "for a decade he is the one who has been asked to carry the burden of social reform, to integrate his schools and his neighborhood, [the one who] has been asked by comfortable people to pay the social debts due to the poor and the black."[20]

As Pete Hamill probed the public's mood during the election campaign of 1968, he concluded that although there were many crosscurrents at work, the dominant one was desperate nostalgia. Americans—poor, working-class, middle-class, and rich—looked back to a year like 1910, said Hamill, himself a son of the post–World War II working class. His parents and his parents' friends longed for a time "when there were harvests in the fall and feasts in the spring, when kids went swimming in the old swimming hole and played baseball and respected God, Flag and Country. Most of all they want to return to a time in America when you lived in the same house all of your life and knew everybody you would ever care to know on the street where you were born."[21]

George Wallace and Richard Nixon understood this sense of longing for the past but were unprepared by temperament and personality for fully exploiting the historical mirage. It was no accident that Ronald Reagan, a veteran of America's nostalgia machine—the movies—instinctively understood how to sell the promise of cultural stability and permanence

19. Marshall Frady, "Gary, Indiana," *Harper's Magazine,* August 1969, p. 37.
20. Peter Schrag, "The Forgotten American," *Harper's Magazine,* August 1969, p. 30.
21. Pete Hamill, "Wallace," *Ramparts,* October 26, 1968, p. 47.

in a time of cultural disintegration and chaos. Writing at the height of the Californian's ascendancy, Garry Wills sought to decode the president's appeal to Americans in the 1980s. The secret, he concluded, lay in Reagan's skills as an actor with limited talent who had learned to "sell himself" effortlessly as a man for all times. Our national identity, Wills argued,

> has to be sought in the past. That is why continued scrutiny of the real past is so important to human growth. . . . The power of . . . [Reagan's] appeal is the great joint confession that we cannot live with our real past, that we not only prefer but need a substitute. . . . He is the ideal past, the successful present, the hopeful future all in one. He is convincing because he has "been there"—been almost everywhere in our modern American culture—yet he "has no past" in the sinister sense. He is guilelessly guiltless. If, to recognize the miracle, one must reject historical record for historical fantasy, fact for parable, it is a small price to pay. . . . [He] has made pretending the easiest thing we do.[22]

Ronald Reagan ended his eight years in office as a remarkably popular figure among white Americans (and an equally unpopular figure among black citizens, who—by a three-to-one majority—agreed with the statement that the president was a racist). But that very popularity allowed him to forgo the grubby manipulation of racial appeals. In practicing to perfection the advice Pat Moynihan had offered to Richard Nixon when he suggested a brief period of "benign neglect" on the race question, Reagan presided over a massive shift in public attitudes away from the compensatory racial and economic policies of the 1960s.

The late spring of 1988 should have been a period of triumph for George Bush. With relative ease, he had routed his main rival for the Republican nomination, Robert Dole, and Ronald Reagan's continued popularity seemed to ensure that the vice-president would not run under the burden that had afflicted Hubert Humphrey when he campaigned with the albatross of LBJ dangling from his neck in 1968.

But the polls were a nightmare. Gallup and Harris showed Bush trailing Michael Dukakis, the likely Democratic nominee, by fifteen to twenty points. GOP tracking polls were even more unnerving: on the critical "lik-

22. Wills, *Reagan's America,* 387.

ability" and "trust" scales, voters were split down the middle on Bush. But 70 percent said they liked Dukakis, and more than 80 percent said they trusted him.

In something of a crisis atmosphere, Vice-President Bush convened a Memorial Day summit meeting at Kennebunkport of his closest political advisers: Lee Atwater, the slashing head of the Republican National Committee, who had played such a pivotal role in the 1980 and 1984 Reagan campaigns; James Baker, White House chief of staff, treasury secretary, and longtime friend to Bush; Stuart Spencer, a Reagan adviser with a reputation for blistering candor; Robert Teeter, a Detroit pollster and retail marketing specialist who had been associated with Republican candidates since the Ford administration; and Roger Ailes, the advertising man picked to handle the Bush campaign (Ailes had single-handedly orchestrated the rescue operation for Reagan after the GOP candidate seemed to collapse in his first 1984 debate with Walter Mondale).

All were men of strong conviction and opinion, but Atwater seized the initiative and shaped the direction of that critical two-day meeting. He knew that George Bush was no Ronald Reagan. No matter how many pork rinds he ate or how much he insisted he loved country music, no amount of gimmickry or media manipulation would lead the American people to embrace the awkward Connecticut-born patrician as one of them or (as in Reagan's case) as a forceful and decisive president straight from central casting. The only hope for winning the election was to destroy Michael Dukakis, a project for which Lee Atwater was temperamentally suited. As one of his friends later bragged, the Atwater thesis of electability was a simple one, best expressed in the language of the drag race: "if you drive the other guy's negatives up high enough, he won't be a credible candidate and you can blow by him."[23]

This, after all, was the South Carolina–born political consultant who pointed with pride to his role in the Floyd Spence–Tom Turnipseed congressional campaign of 1980. Turnipseed, a former George Wallace aide turned liberal, was a popular Democratic state senator who seemed well on his way to defeating the incumbent Republican, Spence. But six days

23. David R. Runkel, ed., *Campaign for President: The Managers Look at '88* (Dover, Mass.: Auburn Publishing Co., 1989), 163.

before the general election, Atwater illegally obtained medical records from the University of North Carolina Hospital showing that Turnipseed, as a teenager, had received shock treatments for depression. He passed the records to a friendly journalist, who then questioned the Democratic candidate at a Columbia news conference about "rumors" of his treatment for mental illness. When Turnipseed angrily charged Atwater with leaking the information, the Republican political operative innocently replied that he would rather not comment on the accusations of "someone who was hooked up to jumper cables." [24]

Negative advertisements were hardly new to politics. In the 1934 California governor's race, Hollywood producers—fearful that the novelist Upton Sinclair, a lifelong socialist, might win—produced a series of visceral film shorts depicting the writer as the tool of Communist/criminal elements intent on taking over the state. Sinclair lost.

But political consultants had made enormous strides in selling soap and politicians since the 1930s. Only seventy-two hours before the Kennebunkport summit meeting, polling specialist Robert Teeter—on Atwater's instructions—assembled thirty voters, ranging in age from twenty-three to sixty-four, in two comfortable rooms at a marketing firm in Paramus, New Jersey. A single characteristic distinguished the carefully selected group from a random sample of voters: all had voted for Ronald Reagan in the past, yet they planned to cast their ballots for Michael Dukakis in November. The group interview, they were told, was designed to explore how much voters knew about the Democratic candidate's career. Although they understood they were being taped, they were not told that the Republican National Committee had financed the exercise. And they were unaware that Atwater, Teeter, Ailes, and two other Bush staff members were watching and listening behind the large two-way mirror on the wall of each room.[25]

The focus-group testing of campaign issues in Paramus was the end

24. Lee Atwater with Todd Brewster, "Lee Atwater's Last Campaign," *Life,* February 1991, p. 64; Author's interview with Tom Turnipseed, July 28, 1988.

25. The most complete account of the experiment is by CBS Washington correspondent Bob Schieffer and writer Gary Paul Gates in their book *The Acting President* (New York: E. P. Dutton, 1989), 358–62. According to Atwater, the other two Bush aides present were Nick Brady and Craig Fuller; Runkel, ed., *Campaign for President,* 111.

product of the more than two decades of conscious manipulation of the electorate, a process in which the Republican Party had an enormous edge. Begun in the Nixon administration, the use of marketing research had moved into high gear after 1976 as the GOP put together a team of battle-hardened media veterans and political consultants with years of experience in running large-scale political campaigns. The Democrats were never able to afford, or to summon, a team that approached the skills of men like Atwater, Ailes, Teeter, and consultants Edward Rodgers and Edward Rollins. Between 1977 and 1984 the various Republican Party committees, led by the National Committee, raised $767 million to the Democrats' $201 million. Since the maintenance of party structure probably cost in excess of $150 million for each party, this huge imbalance gave the GOP a ten-to-one edge in the availability of funds for background research, polling, and the testing of advertising/marketing plans.

Thus, in 1988, at a time when the Democratic Party's research operation consisted of two staffers, a secretary, and five filing cabinets, the Republican National Committee's "Operation Research" division had thirty-five researchers, five data processors, and access to a Cray mainframe computer with more than 125,000 cross-indexed entries on Dukakis. When Atwater outlined the five "attack" issues he planned to use in the 1988 campaign, director of communications Mark Goodin was able to pull together the appropriate quotations from Dukakis within twenty-four hours.

Between 1977 and 1984 the Democratic National Committee raised $186,000 to finance four national polls to obtain a general sense of the public mood. During these same years the Republican National Committee paid Richard Wirthlin's Decision-Making Information an average retainer of more than $100,000 a *month* to chart the most minute shifts in the public mood. Between 1983 and 1984, combined Republican committees spent nearly 9 million on a series of pre-election polls, and then followed these up with highly structured focus-group testing in which marketing firms interviewed voters on their views about various issues in order to structure positive and negative advertisements. The disparities between the two parties for 1988 were nearly as great.[26]

26. Edsall and Edsall, *Chain Reaction,* 210–11. Nor did the disparity change. In 1991,

But even Atwater and Ailes were unprepared for their success in Paramus. After the focus-group participants had settled into comfortable chairs, a carefully trained moderator ran through a list of at-first innocuous, then increasingly controversial, aspects of Dukakis' political career. Almost immediately, the Bush team picked up issues that made the voters uncomfortable. When the moderator explained that Dukakis had opposed the death penalty, several participants expressed surprise and disagreement. They appeared even more disturbed when she told them that the governor had vetoed a bill requiring Massachusetts teachers to lead their students in the Pledge of Allegiance each morning. (She did not explain that the state's attorney general had recommended a veto of the measure on the grounds it was clearly unconstitutional under the Supreme Court's Jehovah's Witness decision of 1943.)

And then, paydirt: The moderator described the Massachusetts prison furlough plan allowing criminals to leave their cells for up to forty-eight hours on weekend passes. In a low-key, conversational tone, she detailed the horrific story of Willie Horton, a black convicted murderer permitted a weekend furlough—his tenth since his conviction a decade earlier—on June 6, 1986. He disappeared. Ten months later, a heavily armed Horton forced his way into a suburban Maryland bungalow, tied up twenty-five-year-old Cliff Barnes, beat and stabbed him, and threw him into the basement. When Barnes's fiancée, Angela Miller, returned home later in the evening, Horton tied her hands behind her back and raped her twice over a four-hour period while the semiconscious Barnes lay listening to her screams.[27]

Even before Dukakis won the nomination, the Republican National Committee's political research group had identified the furlough issue as promising (Tennessee's Albert Gore had raised the Horton case in the New York Democratic primary that spring). But Atwater was astonished by the test group's response to the story of Willie Horton. Fifteen of the thirty

for example, the National Democratic Party—despite its control of both houses of Congress—was able to raise only $4.3 million from business interests (and another $1.2 million from labor unions). The Republican Party pulled in nearly $13 million from business contributions. New York *Times,* May 16, 1992.

27. Robert James Bidinotto, "Getting Away with Murder," *Reader's Digest,* July 1988, pp. 57–63.

voters—said they had changed their minds. They would never vote for Dukakis. Lee Atwater had found his silver bullet.

To base a campaign on the Horton issue posed no problems for Atwater, but the decision should have been difficult for George Bush. The vice-president's family had an impeccable record on civil rights. In 1962 his father, Senator Prescott Bush, cosponsored a strong civil rights measure that was a direct forerunner of the Kennedy legislation. Although the younger Bush opposed the Civil Rights Act of 1964 in his first political campaign against Texas senator Ralph Yarborough, the misstep seemed an aberration in his public career. When he ran for Congress in 1966, he defeated his racially reactionary Democratic opponent in a campaign that appealed for biracial cooperation, and despite the hostility of African Americans to the Republican Party following the Goldwater campaign, Bush carried two-thirds of the black vote in his district. After 1966 he joined forces with moderates in both parties. With liberal GOP congressman Charles Goodell, he proposed a Republican-style alternative to Lyndon Johnson's War on Poverty and introduced legislation for the creation of a $2.5 billion "Human Renewal Fund" to channel capital into the nation's collapsing inner cities.

Over the next decade, George Bush would zig and zag on a number of political issues, but seldom on the question of race. Overall, his voting record placed him squarely in the ranks of the moderate Republicans. He took a key role in family planning in the late 1960s (including a strong position in favor of the right to abortion), and he enthusiastically backed the Nixon administration's Philadelphia Plan, which gave the federal government the authority to require companies and trade unions to set up goals and timetables for hiring and promoting minorities. When he ran against Lloyd Bentsen for a Senate seat in 1970, he described himself as a representative of "modern" Republicanism as he appealed to affluent suburbanites and blacks. After he lost the race, his career throughout the 1970s was dominated by foreign-policy assignments: ambassador to the United Nations, chief of the U.S. diplomatic mission in China, and then director of the Central Intelligence Agency. But his position as a liberal on both social and racial issues remained consistent through the 1980 campaign for the Republican presidential nomination; he supported the Equal Rights Amendment, defended *Roe* v. *Wade,* and reemphasized his commitment to civil rights by publicly apologizing for his opposition to the 1964 Civil Rights Act.

In a sense, the clarifying moment of George Bush's stance on racial issues would seem to have come during his first term in Congress. In April of 1968 a Johnson-backed open-housing bill came up for a vote. The Republican leadership in the House and Senate urged rejection of the measure; polls in Bush's Houston district showed overwhelming opposition—he, in fact, had already declared himself against the measure. But after agonizing through most of the night preceding the final House vote, he broke ranks with the Republican leadership and voted for the Open Housing Act.

When he returned to his home state the following week, he faced a forum of four hundred furious Texans at a suburban west Houston auditorium. "I had you in my house and here you would destroy everything you stood for," a former supporter angrily told him in one of the more temperate attacks on the first-term congressman up for reelection in a hard-fought campaign. After listening for over an hour, Bush responded by acknowledging the concerns of his angry constituents. But he would not back down. In a passionate justification of his vote, he spoke of the hundreds of young veterans—many of them black—who were returning from Vietnam. The idea that "our young people would come back from fighting in Vietnam" and then be told that the government would not protect them in their right to choose where they "could or could not live" was unthinkable, he said. "I would never be able to do that in my whole life. I would die first." It was, by any measure, an authentic profile in courage and conviction. Twenty years later, it was the only incident from his four years in Congress that Bush would mention in his autobiography, *Looking Forward:* "I can truthfully say that nothing I've experienced in public life, before or since, has measured up to the feeling [of satisfaction] I had when I went home that night." Even the hostile Houston audience responded to a rare moment of political courage; at the end of his remarks they gave him a standing ovation.[28]

But when Atwater showed videotaped excerpts from the Paramus, New

28. Jefferson Morley, "Bush and the Blacks: An Unknown Story," *New York Review of Books,* January 16, 1992, p. 23.

Jersey, market test and laid out a campaign strategy that included use of the Horton case, George Bush never hesitated. Two of the group gathered at Kennebunkport told a reporter, off the record, that the candidate expressed concern that the plan might backfire. But that was all. "As far as I could tell he had no qualms about it," said one staff member. "It was just the facts of life. He realized that as far behind as he was it was the only way to win." [29]

The actual execution of the Horton strategy was a textbook operation in the new slash-and-burn politics. Throughout the summer, even before the Democratic convention, Roger Ailes—dubbed the "Darth Vader of political advertising"—released a series of ads attacking the Massachusetts governor. Some, like those emphasizing Dukakis' support for gun control, were carefully restricted to areas of the country where they were "hot" issues; others, like the Pledge of Allegiance commercial or accusations about dirty Boston Harbor, were shown nationwide. [30]

Although these preliminary sorties may have raised questions in the mind of the electorate, Dukakis' superb speech in Atlanta gave him a strong boost; polls showed he had reclaimed the seventeen-point lead he held in late May.

Then came the one-two punch.

During the Democratic convention, right-wing followers of Lyndon H. LaRouche circulated fliers claiming that Dukakis had undergone psychiatric treatment for depression in 1973 and 1978. There was no evidence to support such a rumor, and these were, after all, the same people who insisted that Queen Elizabeth was a dope pusher. But several of Atwater's aides encouraged reporters to look into the story. When the newspeople were unable to uncover any basis for the rumors, the matter died down, only to be reignited when a reporter for one of the LaRouche publications pointedly asked Reagan about the mental-health issue. The president waved off the question with a grin: "I'm not going to pick on an invalid," he said. Even when Dukakis released his medical records and had his personal physician vouch for his mental stability, the rumors had a devastating impact on his campaign. As Susan Estrich, his campaign

29. Schieffer and Gates, *Acting President,* 360.
30. Los Angeles *Times,* October 28, 1988.

manager, pointed out, for the next twenty-four hours every local television show in America was interrupted with a bulletin: "Dukakis not crazy: More at 11."[31] In the following week, support for the Democratic nominee fell by eight points. South Carolina's Tom Turnipseed, who had seen first-hand Atwater's skill at raising "mental health" questions, tried to persuade two reporters to dig into the circumstances surrounding the rumors; neither was interested.[32]

It was time for Willie Horton. George Bush—always emphasizing the name Willie Horton and always linking him with Dukakis—had been discussing the furlough issue as early as the week after his Kennebunkport meeting, first at a meeting before Texas Republicans on June 9, and then before Illinois Republicans a week later. When southern GOP leaders convened that same month, one Georgia Republican described Atwater as almost manic in his glee at the prospect of pairing photos of Dukakis and Jesse Jackson with ads featuring the Horton case. They were going to "strip the bark off the little bastard [Dukakis]," he promised. "For all I know," he added sarcastically, "Willie Horton . . . may end up to be Dukakis' running mate."[33]

Within the Bush campaign there remained lingering fears that an all-out press on the Horton issue would invite charges of racism. In early July, however, the Republicans' carefully targeted Market Opinion Research focus-group sessions began to feature an article on the Horton case in *Reader's Digest*. (Although dismissed by journalists and intellectuals, *Reader's Digest*—with a readership of more than fifteen million—may be the most influential magazine of middle America.) The harrowing account of the ordeal of Cliff Barnes and Angela Miller emphasized the fact that Dukakis had failed to offer any apology to the couple. Although the article did not explicitly identify Horton's race, it described him as a hoodlum from Roxbury, a heavily black area of Boston.[34]

So positive was the group response that Atwater put aside his misgiv-

31. Jack W. Germond and Jules Witcover, *Whose Broad Stripes and Bright Stars: The Trivial Pursuit of the Presidency, 1988* (New York: Warner Books, 1989), 360–61; Runkel, ed., *Campaign for President,* 169.

32. Author's interview with Tom Turnipseed, March 3, 1994.

33. New York *Times,* March 30, 1991; Edsall and Edsall, *Chain Reaction,* 223–24.

34. Germond and Witcover, *Whose Broad Stripes,* 162–64.

ings and, under the aegis of the Bush Re-election Committee, released a hard-hitting television commercial. While a voice-over described the Massachusetts furlough plan as a rogue operation that resulted in the escape of convicted murderers who killed and robbed, a screen graphic showed the number 268 superimposed over a line of plodding convicts who moved in and out of a revolving prison door. In fact, only 4 of the 268 furloughed prisoners who failed to return (out of a total of 13,000 who participated in the program over a twelve-year period) had been convicted of murder, and similar programs existed in thirty-three states (although only four allowed the furlough of murderers)—but accuracy, of course, is quite another issue. The grainy and stylized film clip made it difficult to tell the race of the "prisoners" (actors hired for the ad), and there was no mention of Willie Horton.

By this time, however, it was hardly necessary to point out that Horton was black. Another Republican group called "Americans for Bush"— allegedly acting independently of the Bush Re-election Committee—blanketed Cable News Network with an ad declaring that "Dukakis not only opposed the death penalty, he allowed first-degree murderers to have weekend passes from prison." A bushy-headed—and clearly black—Horton stared dully into the camera. Forty-eight hours after the initial "Americans for Bush" commercial, the California Committee for the Presidency released a second, even more devastating radio ad featuring Cliff Barnes. "Mike Dukakis and Willie Horton changed our lives forever. . . . Horton broke into our home. For twelve hours, I was beaten, slashed and terrorized," he told listeners. "My wife Angie was brutally raped." But when this "liberal experiment" failed, said Barnes, "Dukakis simply looked away." [35]

Dukakis should have been prepared for the storm. After all, a Massachusetts newspaper had won a Pulitzer Prize for detailing the process by which the stubbornly self-righteous governor had stonewalled attempts to change the furlough program after the Horton case. Perhaps encouraged by Mario Cuomo's advice to let it "blow over," Dukakis first ignored the issue and then issued a legalistic statement defending the furlough program.

35. Los Angeles *Times,* October 28, 1988.

When the racial implications of the Horton ad campaign became apparent, Dukakis finally responded and accused the Republicans of racism. His protest, however, seemed to elevate the advertisements to a bona fide news story, and the airwaves quickly filled with news accounts that ran excerpts from the Ailes commercials alongside the photograph of Horton. Thus, the dozens of television news stories on prime time ended up reinforcing what Elizabeth Drew of the *New Yorker* labeled "the most slimy issue I have ever seen in an election." [36] Perhaps, mused political scientist Larry Sabato, all of the free television coverage of the Horton commercial was what George Bush had in mind when he talked about a "thousand points of light." [37]

Atwater and Ailes brushed aside Dukakis' feeble counterattack. Ailes indignantly protested that his commercials did not even mention Horton in connection with the Massachusetts furlough program. And even though a former Ailes employee had filmed the ads using Horton's picture, Ailes (and Atwater) insisted that the national Republican Party had nothing to do with these "independent" ads. When reporters failed to follow up on widespread Washington rumors that the two had secretly coordinated all of the Horton campaigns, Robert Beckel, a former Mondale campaign manager and widely respected Washington political consultant, walked down to the Federal Election Commission office and—in less than two hours—researched the contributors and organizers of "Americans for Bush" and the "Committee for the Presidency." As he suspected, all were closely tied to mainline Republican politics. Hundreds of newspeople were falling all over themselves writing "horse-race" stories about who was behind and who was ahead, a still-angry Beckel remembered two months after the election. "But I couldn't get one lousy newspaper reporter to get

36. Martin Agronsky's *Inside Washington,* ABC Television, October 21, 1988 (Transcript in possession of the author).

37. Los Angeles *Times,* October 28, 1988. In her study of presidential campaign advertising (published after these lectures were given), Kathleen Hall Jamieson amply documents the Atwater-Ailes full-throttle use of the Horton issue, then makes the rather strained argument that this was not "racist" since the "racism that existed in these ads was placed there through complicity with frightened audiences." Precisely. Kathleen Hall Jamieson, *Packaging the Presidency: A History and Criticism of Presidential Campaign Advertising* (New York: Oxford University Press, 1992), 477.

off his duff and explore one of the most important stories in the campaign." Only in the week preceding the election did Elizabeth Drew quote an unnamed source within the Republican National Committee who hinted that the so-called independent committees were coordinating their Horton commercials with the RNC.[38]

Following Bush's uplifting convention performance, the Dukakis campaign seemed to collapse. The vice-president moved ahead by five points in all of the major polls. In twenty-eight days, 12 percent of the electorate had switched candidates, just as the Paramus focus group had predicted. "We could never have done it without Dukakis," Atwater crowed, deriding the pathetically inept Democratic response.[39]

No campaign ever turns on one issue. A constellation of factors underlay the August-September surge of George Bush and the decline of Michael Dukakis—not the least of which were the continuing popularity of Ronald Reagan, the powerful appeal of the vice-president's "no new taxes" pledge, and the general ineptness and rigidity of the Democrats' cautious effort. But no one—*no one*—who followed that campaign believes George Bush had any more devastating ally than the homicidal black rapist Willie Horton.

The Willie Horton ad was a defining moment in the 1988 campaign because of what it tells us about the politics of race. The first thing that should be said is that it worked because it was believable. As Republican political consultant Edward Rollins argued, the ad was effective because it "reinforced the negative impression that people had about Dukakis, that he was a Massachusetts liberal who was against the death penalty and soft on crime."[40]

Second, the ad worked because it was the culmination of twenty years of shifting attitudes in American society. In *Chain Reaction,* Thomas and Mary Edsall argue that George Wallace, Richard Nixon, and Ronald

38. *Inside Washington,* October 21, 1988. One of the best treatments of the Horton issue is found in the transcript of the conference held December 2–4, 1988, by the top campaign staff of the candidates. Atwater and Ailes both denied the connections. The somewhat cynical political operatives who dominated the December conference did not seem convinced. Runkel, ed., *Campaign for President,* 108–29.

39. Los Angeles *Times,* October 28, 1988; New York *Times,* October 17, 1989.

40. Runkel, ed., *Campaign for President,* 126.

Reagan succeeded in convincing a clear majority of the American people that the Democratic Party was out of touch with fundamental American values. Summarized, their thesis is easily caricatured, but essentially it suggests that the Democratic Party in the 1960s had become the party of blacks, of homosexuals, of the undeserving poor, of big-spending bureaucratic defenders of the welfare state, and of those unwilling to defend American interests abroad. And the Republican Party had been able to hammer home this characterization by skillfully representing the growing conservatism of Americans on a number of important "social" issues not directly connected to questions of race: school prayer, criminal defendants' rights, obscenity, and abortion.

Yet race seemed to be the glue that held it all together. For in the issue of blackness is found the same silver bullet that Lee Atwater sought in the 1988 campaign. It has been an easy case to make because of the paralysis of the Democratic Party's leadership. Unwilling to make their case on the basis of pocketbook issues and well aware that such racial and social issues split the major elements of the old New Deal, Democrats stumbled along, offering few alternatives to the rising GOP challenge.

The Democrats may wish it would go away, the Edsalls conclude, but there is ample evidence that a broad public consensus has emerged in which—whatever theoretical opposition to racism may exist—Americans instinctively believe that the black community is marked by higher rates of crime and illegitimacy, a weakened family structure, low achievement in educational levels, and greater demands on the welfare system. And the Democratic Party will do nothing except continue the policies of the past. As one indiscreet GOP campaign official said gleefully in the 1988 campaign, every time Michael Dukakis appeared on a platform with Jesse Jackson, the Republican votes started coming up like change on a cash register. The issue of race remained the driving wedge of American conservative politics.[41]

The Horton ad was a defining moment because of what it tells us about the changing nature of the political system. As our mass-consumption economy moves increasingly toward a service economy, the business of

41. In a sense, the Edsalls' book may serve the same function for the Democratic Party that Kevin Phillips' *Emerging Republican Majority* did for the Republicans in the 1970s.

merchandising, of "packaging the product," of creating an image that will attract the consumer becomes an end in itself. Television, of course, is the ideal medium for the new intellectual order. As one irascible traditionalist has complained, where the "printed work of literature was stable and durable, available in fixed form for rereading, the electronic image floats, transitory and infinitely recombinable in new configurations. Where the dense literary verbal text, gone over again and again, encouraged complex readings, the TV image is direct and literally superficial—*i.e.,* what it is on the surface."

We can judge our culture by the men and women who are our heroes. As a group, they are more likely to be entertainers than entrepreneurs, athletes than intellectuals (or even politicians). In the case of athletes there may be some tenuous link to actual performance. Former Chicago lineman Dick Butkus can prance across a television sound stage touting a he-man's after-shave lotion because, over a ten-year career, he proved his manliness by his ability to drive 250-pound running backs six inches into the turf of a dozen different NFL stadiums. Most public figures today, however, are simply a composite of our infinitely manipulable imagination.

The very essence of modern advertising is a certain carelessness with the truth. Whatever its olfactory virtues, "Passion" is a best-selling per-fume because advertisers have forged an imaginary link between the pur-chaser and the intangible glamour and beauty—the aura—of Elizabeth Taylor. Madonna is a celebrity, not because she can sing on pitch or act, but because we *decide* she is a celebrity. Reality becomes whatever we wish it to be.

At some point, of course, the line between politics and the merchan-dising of celebrity status was crossed. Historians and political scientists debate the exact point of transition; after all, politicians from the earliest days of our democracy have been concerned with projecting an "image" for their constituents. Abraham Lincoln was long since a successful and well-to-do Illinois attorney when his followers (with no discouragement from him) continued to describe their candidate as a "rail-splitter" and to point to his birth in a Kentucky log cabin. Franklin Roosevelt was a master of controlling the public's perception of him. Dwight Eisenhower hired one of Hollywood's best-known actors to advise him on his speeches and public presentations. But the most dramatic shift seems to have taken place in the 1960s, with John Kennedy's masterful and apparently effortless manipulation of television in his 1960 campaign and in his brief presidency.

By the end of the 1980s, however, a quantitative shift had reached the point of a qualitative change. Symbols have always shaped our political process, but these symbols were embedded within a stable system of political parties, stronger cultural traditions, and interconnected institutions. Most of all, there was the assumption that there was some genuine connection between symbols and reality.

Today, television dependency has completed the process in which isolated voters are thrust into a shapeless political landscape dominated by "photo-ops" and subliterate thirty-second (or shorter) commercials that seek to sell a product—in this case a politician—with a series of symbols cynically designed to arouse powerful emotional reflexes. Patriotism: waving fields of grain and rippling American flags and music that tugs your throat. Family: fathers and mothers and towheaded kids, with an occasional black or brown skin thrown in for balance. Fear: shadowy criminal figures lurking in the dark, or shuttered American factories with a hint of the Yellow Peril (or the Brown Peril) thrown in—set to an undercurrent of brooding music.

Even race. For thirty years, most respectable candidates preferred to leave the explicit manipulation of racial fears to politicians like George Wallace who operated on the periphery of American politics. But that line has been eroding since the Ailes ads of the 1988 campaign. In several high-profile races at the beginning of the 1990s, candidates reached down into the grab bag of racial fears to drum up votes. In Louisiana, former Ku Klux Klan leader David Duke, a state representative who had gained the gubernatorial nomination of the Louisiana Republican Party, finished second to Edwin Edwards in Louisiana's open primary, edging out incumbent governor Buddy Roemer; Duke lost to Edwards by a 61-39 margin in the runoff but received 55 percent of the white vote. In Alabama, Republican Guy Hunt won reelection to the governorship after repeatedly linking his Democratic opponent with black leaders through television advertisements.[42] And North Carolina senator Jesse Helms showed how

42. New York *Times,* November 5, 1990.

devastating racial fears could be in his campaign against Harvey Gantt, a black former mayor of Charlotte who had drawn strong support from white voters. Against the surprisingly popular Gantt, Helms used the race issue at every turn, most powerfully in a television ad in which a white worker crumpled a job rejection letter to the accompaniment of a somber voice: "You were qualified for that job, but it had to go to a minority because of quotas."[43]

And sex, of course—preferably allegations of illicit sex involving an opponent. Here it seems unnecessary for political candidates to soil their hands; the news media—and not just the supermarket tabloids, either— have taken care of that. In 1988, when Washington *Post* reporter Paul Taylor asked Democratic presidential aspirant Gary Hart if he had committed adultery, his question (and the media frenzy that followed) toppled the last barriers between public service and private life.[44] It is difficult to say which sight is most unsettling: the presumptuousness of entertainment talk-show hosts asking presidential candidates about their sex lives, the spectacle of candidates earnestly answering these questions, or the breathless enthusiasm with which an audience of political "consumers" tots up their responses.

If "news" is simply another form of entertainment, a commodity to be sold like any other, is it surprising that viewers—and voters—find it increasingly hard to distinguish between the *CBS Evening News* and *Entertainment Tonight?* Between the supermarket tabloids and the Atlanta *Constitution?*

In an attempt to woo black constituents after the divisive Willie Horton ads of the 1988 campaign, the Republican National Committee turned for advice to the Nathan Group Inc. The black political consulting firm urged the president to become more publicly involved in events and activities associated with the black community and specifically to "attend significant

43. Peter Applebome, "Pit Bull Politician," *New York Times Magazine,* October 28, 1990, pp. 35–37; New York *Times,* November 5, 1990.

44. Taylor initially defended his decision to ask the "big A" question, but he later came to have second thoughts. "Our cynicism begets their fakery," he has concluded, "and their fakery begets our cynicism." "The Talk of the Town," *New Yorker,* February 12, 1996, p. 26. Taylor's misgivings are increasingly shared by thoughtful journalists. See particularly James Fallows, *Breaking the News.*

black events such as speaking at major black institutions." But it was not necessary to compromise a "single plank in the Republican Platform" in dealing with blacks. "In politics, perceptions are the only reality," the Nathan Group concluded. "The only thing that's going to count when black Americans consider the merits of the Republican Party is how their perceptions have been molded, negatively or positively." [45]

When such tactics work (and they are not always successful by any means), Democrats are likely to see these developments as a disaster for their party. As the political ground shifts, however, astute practitioners of the art of political manipulation are likely to operate on a bipartisan basis. Politicians, like soldiers, develop their tactics by studying past campaigns. By the time George Bush took office in 1989, future Democratic presidential aspirants were taking notes on the passivity of Michael Dukakis. Attack ads, attack politics are the wave of the future, and any candidate who hopes to survive must learn the requisite political skills for the 1990s: never apologize, never explain, always seize the initiative with slogans that connect emotionally with the voter.

At this moment in our history, a few winds push in the opposite direction. The very cynicism with which political handlers have attempted to manipulate voters has led to a modest backlash. And we can take heart from the fact that hard times have sometimes focused the minds of the American people. Still, pessimist that I am, I cannot help but remember George Orwell's *Nineteen Eighty-four* and the haunting fear of Winston Smith that the past had been destroyed because Big Brother's all-powerful Party could manipulate the record of that past and thus "thrust its hand into the past and say of this or that event, *it never happened.*"

What does it say of our time, that his was not the ultimate nightmare? In the last few years we have learned the limitations of totalitarian regimes, only to face the prospect of a far worse fate in our own political and intellectual culture: the moment at which both politician and voter accept the ultimate lie that "perceptions are the only reality."

"You believe," said O'Brien—the master of Big Brother's torture chamber—that "reality is something objective, external, existing in its own right. . . . But I tell you, Winston, that reality is not external. Reality exists

45. New York *Times,* June 9, 1991.

in the human mind and nowhere else." Tortured and broken, Winston Smith accepted his interrogator's argument: "Anything could be true." The so-called laws of nature were nonsense; gravity was pure invention. Attempting to resist Big Brother, he had tried to fall back on the outmoded notion that there was a "real" world—that words, texts, ideas, had some connection to that reality. But of course there was no such thing. "All happenings are in the mind. Whatever happens in all minds, truly happens."

Dissecting the 1988 campaign, PBS newswoman Judy Woodruff asked Roger Ailes about the possibility of having a candidate who simply decided: "I want to run for president because I want to do something for this country." Before she had finished her question, Ailes erupted in derisive laughter. That's "suicide," he said. Confronted with complaints about the nasty and negative race, Lee Atwater dismissed them as hopelessly naïve and sentimental: "We had only one goal in the campaign: to help elect George Bush. That's the purpose of any political campaign. What other function should a campaign have?" [46]

Forty years ago—it seems several lifetimes ago—Adlai Stevenson earnestly explained his deepest convictions about the calling of the politician. It was often not a very elevating experience, he said, but there had to be a sense at the end of a political campaign that the struggle was more than a question of who won and who lost. Winning might be everything in sports, but in the struggle to understand, to instruct, and to listen to the voice of the people, there had to be some connection between means and ends. The "perception that you can pay too great a price for victory—that the means you use may destroy the principles you think you cherish—is fundamental to democratic responsibility." If the "only way I can get elected is by pandering to people's fears and hatreds," Stevenson told a friend, "I want no part of it." [47]

By the 1990s, Stevenson's earnest disquisition seemed as out of date as bathtub gin and hula hoops. But Stevenson was correct in insisting that

---

46. Runkel, ed., *Campaign for President*, 136; New York *Times*, March 30, 1991.

47. Walter Johnson *et al.*, eds., *Toward a New America, 1955–1957* (Boston: Little, Brown & Co., 1976), 259, Vol. VI of Johnson *et al.*, eds., *The Papers of Adlai E. Stevenson*, 8 vols.

there was a connection between means and ends, a link between campaigning and governing. Politics, argued the Roman moralist and biographer Plutarch, is not "like an ocean voyage or a military campaign, something to be done with some particular end in view, something which leaves off as soon as that end is reached. . . . It is a way of life." The ingredients that make good campaigns increasingly make poor governance. As the chasm between fantasy and reality opens too wide to be bridged by the artful devices of Madison Avenue, the real losers are neither Democrats nor Republicans, but an increasingly cynical and confused electorate primed to switch wildly from one political patent-medicine salesman to another, receding deeper into passivity with each election, and accepting the notion that this nation is ungovernable.

4 | THE POLITICS OF RIGHTEOUSNESS

Chastened by the defeat of Michael Dukakis, few of the obvious contenders for the Democratic nomination seemed eager to challenge a president who had just vanquished Saddam Hussein and captured a 79-percent approval rating from the nation's voters. Within weeks after his formal announcement in the fall of 1991, Bill Clinton moved ahead of his rivals. In his six terms as Arkansas governor, the former Rhodes scholar had earned a reputation as an informed and innovative policy maker with a finely tuned sense of the politically possible. Unlike Dukakis, who had appeared to regard appealing for votes as a necessary, but distasteful, obligation, Clinton reveled in the more mundane demands of campaigning; by 1991 he claimed to have shaken hands with half the voters in Arkansas.[1]

However, a youthful Clinton had avoided the draft; he had even demonstrated against the war in Vietnam as a student at Oxford. A penchant for appointing liberals such as Arkansas public health director Jocelyn Elder offended conservatives in his home state, and his wife's outspoken advocacy of liberal causes annoyed traditionalists. At the same time, he often disappointed supporters by reversing himself when his political

1. John Brummett, *Highwire: From the Backroads to the Beltway—The Education of Bill Clinton* (New York: Hyperion, 1994); Charles F. Allen and Jonathan Portis, *The Comeback Kid: The Life and Career of Bill Clinton* (New York: Carol Publishing Group, 1992); John Hohenberg, *The Bill Clinton Story: Winning the Presidency* (Syracuse, N.Y.: Syracuse University Press, 1994).

future seemed threatened. Most critically, in the new age of tabloid politics, Bill Clinton had a well-earned reputation for womanizing. In short,
he seemed an ideal target for the kind of ads that had shredded the hapless
Dukakis.

But Clinton's first critical decision—hiring James Carville as his top
political consultant—showed he had learned from the mistakes of the
Democratic Party's 1988 nominee. The fast-talking Louisiana Cajun had
gained recognition as a "brass-knuckles kind of guy" in the 1986 Pennsylvania governor's race, when he ran Democrat Robert Casey's campaign
against the popular (and moderate) Republican lieutenant-governor, William Scranton III. With Casey far behind in the polls, Carville mounted
a series of relentless attacks on Scranton. When the Republican nominee
flanked the Democrats by calling for a moratorium on negative campaigning, Casey accepted the challenge. But secretly, Carville retaliated by
planting a rumor that the Casey campaign intended to run a television ad
accusing Scranton of using drugs when he was a college student (Scranton
had readily acknowledged experimenting with marijuana when he was in
college).

Reporters confronted Carville outside his headquarters and demanded,
"Is there a drug spot?"

"Let me tell you something." he replied. "Mr. Casey said no, that he'd
given his word. There are some people that wanted to do it but he said
that he was a person of his word. *So we are not going to run a spot attacking
Bill Scranton for using drugs.*"[2]

Stories praising Casey for refusing to take the political low road blanketed the news; meanwhile—Carville gleefully recalled eight years later—
"'drugs' and 'Scranton' were in the same sentence in people's minds."[3]
To reinforce the message, Carville put together what he called the "guru"
ad. As sitar music twanged in the background, the television camera closed
in on a college picture of Scranton wearing "long hair, beard, scruffy-
looking sixties clothes." The ad never mentioned drugs, explained Carville
slyly. "What it said, though not in so many words, was that Scranton was
a hippie."[4]

    2. Mary Matalin and James Carville, with Peter Knobler, *All's Fair: Love, War, and
Running for President* (New York: Simon & Schuster/Random House, 1994), 38.
    3. *Ibid.*
    4. *Ibid.*, 40.

Down at one time by 15 percentage points, Casey won by 2. Carville had made his reputation as the Democrats' answer to Lee Atwater.

Watching the passing of a law, like watching the making of sausage, is no occupation for the squeamish, warned Theodore Roosevelt. He might have said as much for the presidential campaign of 1992.[5] By January, most political bookmakers had settled on Bill Clinton as the odds-on choice to win the Democratic nomination. To reverse the economic slow-down that had marked the last half of Bush's administration, the hand-some Arkansan proposed a tax cut targeted specifically at the middle class. In addition, he promised bold reforms in health care, welfare, and political campaign financing. The cost of his tax cut and new programs seemed inconsistent with his promise to move the nation toward a balanced budget, but Clinton managed to stay on the offensive against attacks from Republicans and rivals from his own party, insisting that he was a "new" Democrat, more centrist and sensitive to mainstream political views.

Late that month, however, the *Star,* a supermarket tabloid that usually specialized in UFO abductions, released an advance copy of its February 4 issue, featuring Gennifer Flowers, a part-time country-music backup singer and secretary who claimed that she had carried on a twelve-year affair with Bill Clinton. The tabloid, which—according to the *Wall Street Journal*—had paid Flowers more than $130,000, followed up her accusa-tions with a New York press conference featuring the young woman and a ten-minute excerpt from tapes she had secretly made of conversations with the Arkansas governor. Although the tapes contained no information to support her contention she was Clinton's mistress, they seemed to sup-port her argument that the two were considerably more than casual ac-quaintances. The press conference, broadcast live on the Cable News Net-work, finally dissolved in chaos when a radio stringer stammered, "Did the governor use a condom?"[6]

---

5. Although a number of works have been written on the 1992 campaign, none more insightfully describes the transformation in Democratic "media control" than Los Angeles *Times* reporter Tom Rosensteil's *Strange Bedfellows: How Television and the Presidential Candidates Changed American Politics, 1992* (New York: Hyperion, 1993).

6. Clinton staffers insisted that the tapes had been doctored, and the *Star,* after playing excerpts for newsmen, refused to allow an independent laboratory to examine the copy or the originals. Allen and Portis, *Comeback Kid,* 187–94.

A week later, the *Wall Street Journal* published an article describing how Clinton had avoided the draft in 1969 by joining the Reserve Officer Training Corps, then resigning after he received a "safe" number in the draft lottery.[7]

Look on the bright side, James Carville told dispirited campaign staffers. No one was "going to cover a Tom Harkin press conference when you had Stuttering John asking Gennifer Flowers if Bill Clinton wore a rubber."[8]

Within hours of the *Star*'s revelations, Carville had ordered a series of focus-group sessions. Even though Americans might be mesmerized by the scandal, discovered Clinton pollster Stan Greenberg, they were also slightly embarrassed by their prurient fascination and appalled by the trashiness of Clinton's accuser. ("She looks like a liar," said one woman in a focus group. "And she ought to learn to dye her roots.")[9]

Although aides later insisted that the Arkansas governor and his wife needed no coaching, over the course of several "prep" sessions the Clintons picked up valuable insights from Greenberg and his staff. Participants in the focus groups felt comfortable with a generic admission by the presidential candidate that he had encountered "some problems" with his marriage (so long as his wife stood by him and supported him). But anything more "intimate" or detailed made the group uncomfortable and "more involved than they wanted to be."[10] On CBS' *Sixty Minutes,* broadcast at the conclusion of the Super Bowl and watched by more than eighty million Americans, Clinton denied Flowers' story, then continued: "I have acknowledged wrongdoing. I have acknowledged causing pain in my marriage."

"I'm not sitting here because I'm some little woman standing by my man like Tammy Wynette," Hillary Clinton told the interviewer. "I'm sitting here because I love him and I respect him and I honor what he's been through and what we've been through together."[11]

7. *Wall Street Journal,* February 6, 1972.

8. Matalin and Carville, *All's Fair,* 113.

9. *Ibid.*

10. Elizabeth Kolbert, "Test-Marketing a President," *New York Times Magazine,* August 30, 1992, p. 60.

11. Allen and Portis, *Comeback Kid,* 192.

"Just don't call her [Gennifer Flowers] a whore," Carville told his aides; "short of that, let 'er rip." [12] Skillfully, the Clinton staffers played on reporters' guilt over their failure to challenge the 1988 Bush campaign's flag-factory photo-ops and Willie Horton commercials, as well as over the media's descent into tabloid journalism. After a particularly raucous press conference in which shouting newspeople demanded more graphic details on the nature of Clinton's "wrongdoing," Carville accused the press corps of addiction to the "crack cocaine" of contemporary journalism. "Y'all are saying"—he mimicked their distress—"'I want to get off it, we don't want to cover this. Gee, we hate this.'" But "look at your crotch," he sneered, "and there's a big wet splotch there." [13]

Clinton lashed out in more elevated tones. As reporters continued to follow the Gennifer Flowers story and pressed for explanations of inconsistencies in Clinton's accounts of when and how he avoided the draft, the embattled candidate accused the media of deliberately distracting the voters by ignoring the nation's serious economic problems and encouraging the "politics of division and distraction and destruction." [14]

Receptive voters embraced attacks on the media. When Phil Donahue invited Clinton to his morning talk show and demanded that he be more candid about his past "indiscretions," the audience shouted down the popular television host. [15]

Encouraged by his success on the Donahue show and on various radio talk forums, Clinton began to bypass traditional news outlets, skillfully exploiting the new "life-style" programming that had come to dominate broadcasting. During the month of June, he appeared on all three network breakfast shows, Larry King's nationwide radio interview show, MTV, and the late-night Arsenio Hall show (where he donned sunglasses and accompanied the studio orchestra on his saxophone). [16] Despite the

12. Matalin and Carville, *All's Fair,* 113.

13. And if "we're going to vote for the guy that has the biggest flag," said Carville, "the guy that owns the used car lot would win every election." *Ibid.,* 307.

14. James Ceaser and Andrew Busch, *Upside Down and Inside Out: The 1992 Elections and American Politics* (Lanham, Md.: Rowman & Littlefield, 1993), 62–63.

15. Rosensteil, *Strange Bedfellows,* 166.

16. F. Christopher Arterton, "Campaign '92: Strategies and Tactics of the Candidates," in Gerald M. Pomper *et al., The Election of 1992: Reports and Interpretations* (Chatham, N.J.: Chatham House, 1993), 91.

pounding he had taken in the spring primaries, he moved inexorably toward his party's nomination.

When Lee Atwater died from brain cancer in March of 1991, Bush lost his political right arm. With the White House staff in disarray, the president seemed unable to focus on the economic apprehensions of voters or to craft a consistent attack on Clinton. The public seemed to have forgotten the euphoria with which they had greeted returning veterans of Operation Desert Storm. As the economy turned downward in 1991 and unemployment increased, the plight of blue-collar workers worsened and middle-class and upper-middle-class voters suddenly faced the prospect of shrinking wages or layoffs. A popular bumper sticker seemed to sum up the growing disenchantment: "Saddam Hussein Still Has a Job: Do You?" Political pundits complained that Bush could not articulate what he called "the vision thing."

In part, the president was distracted by assaults from the right flank of his own party. During the 1970s and 1980s, politically active right-wing televangelists had laid the foundations for building a permanent home in the Republican Party for the peculiar moral intensity and social agenda of born-again evangelicals.[17] Fund-raiser Richard Viguerie reaped millions of dollars for conservative religious and political groups by dramatizing the threat "liberal Democratic secularism" posed to traditional "family values." Crime and law and order, school prayer, and opposition to abortion had been hot issues since the mid-1960s, but Viguerie and other right-wing publicists were able to up the take of their fund-raising campaigns by escalating the rhetoric. Abortion was not simply a violation of the sanctity of human life: it meant "killing a living baby . . . with burning deadly chemicals or a powerful machine that sucks and tears the little infant from its mother's womb."

With the growing perception of AIDS as a public health crisis and the cultural "coming out" of America's homosexual community, defenders of traditional values found a new target for their fears. "When the homosexuals burn the Holy Bible in public . . . , how can I stand by silently," began a letter Viguerie mailed out in support of singer Anita Bryant's Save Our

17. John Green and James Guth, "The Christian Right in the Republican Party," *Journal of Politics*, L (1988), 150–65.

Children, Inc. "Do you realize what they want? They want to recruit our school children under the protection of the laws of our land!" [18]

Even though Reagan had soft-pedaled the "social" agenda after election day, he had retained the support of the new religious right. These new GOP-Christian soldiers had voted for Bush in 1988, but they never fully trusted a politician who had endorsed freedom of choice as late as 1980, embracing the prolife cause only when he became Reagan's vice-president. Nor did economic conservatives ever forget that it was Republican candidate George Bush who had dismissed Ronald Reagan's 1980 fiscal proposals as "voodoo economics."

The fears of economic and social conservatives seemed borne out in the first three years of the Bush administration. The president antagonized the religious right when he refused to endorse a Jesse Helms proposal to ban "obscene" art from support by the National Endowment for the Arts.[19] Then, in 1990, he abandoned his read-my-lips-no-new-taxes pledge and agreed to a modest bipartisan tax increase to stem the hemorrhaging budget deficits he had inherited from his predecessor. His reluctant decision the following year to sign a Civil Rights Act he had initially derided as a "quota bill" proved the last straw for former Nixon aide Patrick Buchanan. The right-wing columnist and television personality announced his candidacy just ten weeks before the New Hampshire primary election and pledged to represent the core Republican constituency of die-hard, low-tax conservatives and social "moralists" who wanted no compromise on abortion, gun control, gay rights, and school prayer. Although Buchanan's most effective television ads ridiculed Bush's read-my-lips pledge, he soon began to push other hot-button racial and "moral" issues.

As part of the Nixon White House, Buchanan had been one of George Wallace's biggest ideological fans. Now he showed what he had learned from the Alabama campaigner as he excoriated what he called the "whole rotten infrastructure of reverse discrimination" and lashed out at the "professional civil rights agitators." He contrasted the idyllic Connecticut Avenue of his Washington youth with the current noisy sidewalks filled with

18. Alan Crawford, *Thunder on the Right: The "New Right" and the Politics of Resentment* (New York: Pantheon, 1980), 52.
19. New York *Times,* March 23, 1990.

"these guys playing bongo drums," and he seemed genuinely obsessed by the threat a growing "pederast proletariat" posed to the nation's moral integrity.

Buchanan's take-no-prisoners campaign style was best reflected in the notorious antihomosexual commercial he used in the Georgia Republican primary. The thirty-second television ad showed gay black men in chains and leather harnesses dancing in slow motion while a grim-voiced announcer identified the footage as part of a film funded by the Bush administration's National Endowment for the Arts in order to glorify homosexuality, pornography, and blasphemy.[20]

Although Buchanan never drew more than 37 percent of the vote in any Republican primary, he forced the president to placate the right wing of his party. (After Buchanan's strong showing in New Hampshire, Bush unceremoniously fired the head of the National Endowment for the Arts.) Desperate to shore up the party's right wing, the president and his campaign aides gave ultraconservatives center stage at the Republican nominating convention in Houston.

The 1992 platform promised that the GOP would defend the nation's "Judeo-Christian heritage" against a Democratic Party that was waging a "guerrilla war against American values." The election would not be a struggle between policy alternatives, televangelist Pat Robertson told the cheering delegates, but a contest between a Republican Party upholding moral "family" values and a Clinton Democratic Party committed to "a radical plan to destroy the traditional family and transfer its function to the federal government."

Vice-President Dan Quayle's wife, Marilyn, attacked Bill and Hillary Clinton for their 1960s "counterculture" values. Remember, she told her wildly enthusiastic audience, "not everyone demonstrated, dropped out, took drugs, joined in the sexual revolution or dodged the draft." The division between Republicans and Democrats was more than a struggle between "conservative" and "liberal" ideologies, agreed her husband.

---

20. As journalists Jack Germond and Jules Witcover pointed out, this accusation was a "bit of a stretch." The NEA had given a general grant to the American Film Institute, which had, in turn, given a regrant to the Rocky Mountain Film Institute, which had, in turn, given the film maker $5,000. Jack W. Germond and Jules Witcover, *Mad as Hell: Revolt at the Ballot Box* (New York: Warner Books, 1992), 233–36.

Americans had a choice between a Republican Party that was "fighting for what is right" and a Democratic Party that refused "to see what is wrong."

But it was Patrick Buchanan who delivered the most memorable lines of the convention: "My friends, this election is about more than who gets what. It is about who we are. It is about what we believe and what we stand for as Americans. There is a religious war going on in this country for the soul of America. It is a cultural war as critical to the kind of nation we shall be as the Cold War itself. And in that struggle for the soul of America, [Bill] Clinton and [Hillary] Clinton are on the other side and George Bush is on our side." [21]

A *Newsweek* poll showed that Bush's standing had gone up only three points after the convention. Most observers, including a fair number of Republicans, saw the events in Houston as a disaster for a president starting out his reelection campaign. [22] But the GOP nominee and his top staffers had all read an advance copy of Buchanan's speech; not one had raised a red flag over his apocalyptical rhetoric. "We did not understand the impact of that speech," acknowledged Mary Matalin, political director of the Bush campaign. Matalin saw it primarily as a matter of poor tactics. The Republican high command should have seen "how the Democrats could distort and misinterpret Buchanan's speech, and, more important, the media's shift in focus to it." [23] After the election was over, pollster Robert Teeter defended the Buchanan-Robertson speeches as a necessary step in shoring up the core constituency of the Republican Party. "The mistake we made in the convention," agreed GOP strategist Charles Black, was losing "control of spin." [24]

James Carville supported this interpretation. It was a myth that the

---

21. *Ibid.,* 410.

22. Ralph Reed, executive director of the Christian Coalition, argues that the convention was a strong plus for Bush and claims that it narrowed Clinton's lead from twenty-one to five points, but the largest "bounce" I have found in a major poll is seven points. Ralph Reed, *Politically Incorrect: The Emerging Faith Factor in American Politics* (Dallas: Word Books, 1994), 110; Howard Fineman and Ann McDaniel, "Bush: What Bounce?" *Newsweek,* August 31, 1992, p. 26; New York *Times,* August 22, 1994.

23. Matalin and Carville, *All's Fair,* 303–305.

24. Germond and Witcover, *Mad as Hell,* 413.

Republicans alienated large numbers of voters with their harsh rhetoric, he later wrote. Most voters angered by the hyped-up "family values" speeches were already planning to vote against Bush. Focus groups and postconvention polling by the Democrats showed that most swing voters were apprehensive about the economy. By failing to "define themselves economically," the convention had reinforced the public's impression that the president was drifting.[25]

Building upon the experience of the Bush-Dukakis campaign, the Republican National Committee put together an "opposition research" team of several dozen to dig out information on Clinton, and furnished them with the latest technology, including an upgraded CD-ROM information bank. Staffers boasted that their computer was filled with data ranging from the Democrat's high-school-yearbook prophecy to his most recent newspaper coverage, as well as every television appearance he had ever made. They also had summaries, supporting documents, and audio and film clips on every negative statement made about the governor of Arkansas.[26] "Going negative," said Mary Matalin after the smoke of the 1992 battle had cleared, fostered a "creative mood" for political campaigners and their staffs. It was a "much more psychically rewarding challenge to slash the opposition than to cobble together another round of gushy, flag-waving, isn't-our-guy-great ads."[27]

One ad proposed by the Bush campaign opened at the Vietnam Memorial. A voice-over mused aloud, wondering whether some of these heroes had died because Clinton avoided the draft. The sequence ended with footage of World War II aviator Bush being fished from the sea after his plane had been shot down. But Democrats placed Bush's advertising team on the defensive by constantly berating reporters for their failure in 1988 to challenge the racist overtones of the Willie Horton ad. And in late July, Mary Matalin learned just how the ground rules had changed.

When Republican focus groups showed Clinton to be most vulnerable on issues of "trust" and "character," Matalin began releasing a series of "Clinton Lie-a-Day" fax attacks, usually referring to the Arkansas gov-

25. Matalin and Carville, *All's Fair,* 306.
26. New York *Times,* May 7, 1992.
27. Matalin and Carville, *All's Fair,* 227.

ernor as "slick Willie." After one fax detailing Clinton's problems in dealing with "bimbo eruptions," a New York *Times* reporter asked if her tactics did not violate the president's promise to avoid personal attacks. They were simply pointing to the "larger issue," responded Matalin. Clinton was "evasive and slick. We've never said to the press that he's a philandering, pot-smoking draft dodger." [28]

Putting negative stories in circulation by denying responsibility for them is a classic political maneuver; Richard Nixon was a master at this kind of drive-by slander. But this time it backfired. After television and newspaper journalists hammered away at what seemed to be the transparent duplicity of her strategy, Matalin had to issue a halfhearted apology. (She claimed her outburst was totally spontaneous and stemmed from exhaustion rather than calculation.) Campaign advisers reluctantly decided to shelve a number of anti-Clinton spots, including the Vietnam Memorial ad. Attack commercials still dominated the Bush campaign, but there would be no 1992 silver bullet equivalent to the Willie Horton ad. [29] The Democrats had "carefully laid on the media the definition that we were the most despicable, negative, lowlife, cretinous, slimehead campaigners God ever created," Matalin complained, until it became an "article of faith in the press, and therefore the country, that Republicans were negative campaigners." [30]

Notable for its absence in 1992 was any overt discussion of racial issues. On April 29, in the midst of the presidential primaries, a suburban Los Angeles jury acquitted four policemen of the beating of black motorist Rodney King. Although an onlooker had videotaped the prolonged assault on an unarmed King, attorneys for the policemen convinced a suburban jury of ten whites, one Asian American, and one Hispanic that King was "in charge" of the confrontation and had provoked his own beating.

28. *Ibid.*, 270.

29. In his study of the television coverage of the 1992 campaign, Tom Rosenstiel found that 75 percent of the Bush ads were attacks on Clinton, but the Democrats were not dramatically different: nearly 50 percent of their twenty-four major television commercials were attacks on George Bush. Rosensteil, *Strange Bedfellows,* 289–93.

30. In fact, it was not just the Democrats who decried the campaign's negativity; even Lee Atwater, on his deathbed, repented of using the Horton ad. Lee Atwater, with Todd Brewster, "Lee Atwater's Last Campaign," *Life,* February, 1991, pp. 64–65.

South central Los Angeles erupted in one of the most destructive riots in modern American history. Fifty-eight people died and another two thousand suffered injuries, while raging fires and widespread looting led to nearly $750 million in property damage.[31]

Each party initially tried to place the issue in a partisan context. Clinton blamed the violence on Republican policies that had ignored racial divisions and fostered "more than a decade of urban decay."[32] Bush shot back that the riot had nothing to do with protests against injustice, it had been "the brutality of [the] mob, pure and simple." According to White House spokesman Marlin Fitzwater, the riots were "the result of the Great Society programs of the 1960s and 1970s."[33] But the race issue quickly dropped from the electoral screen. The King beating, acquittal, and riot had "forced more insulated Americans to look, briefly, at the ravaged ground and human desperation of the inner city," concluded one observer of the 1992 presidential campaign. But the "sight was so dreadful that most Americans were happy to turn to something else."[34]

Still, an awareness of racial issues remained just below the surface, particularly for Democratic strategists. Everyone on Clinton's staff knew the figures by heart: beginning with the election of Ronald Reagan in 1980, the white male vote had favored Republican candidates by nearly three to two, while white women narrowly supported Democratic nominees.[35] Although many factors contributed to this gender gap, most studies pointed to the critical importance of race. In 1985 Democratic pollster Stan Greenberg had conducted a number of focus-group interviews in Macomb County, Michigan, a white suburb of Detroit, the home of the archetypal "Reagan Democrat." One after another of the white male voters interviewed lashed out at what they saw as the Democratic Party's capitulation to black demands.[36] Greenberg became Clinton's chief pollster in the 1992 campaign. Although he agreed with the importance of focusing on eco-

31. Los Angeles *Times*, May 11, 1992.

32. New York *Times*, May 1, 1992.

33. New York *Times*, May 2, 1992.

34. Wilson Carey McWilliams, "The Meaning of the Election," in Pomper *et al.*, *Election of 1992*, p. 203.

35. New York *Times*, November 5, 1992.

36. Kolbert, "Test-Marketing a President," 21.

nomic issues, he constantly reminded the Arkansas governor and his staff that they had to make a special effort to regain these white male voters.

The Democratic candidate knew that Michael Dukakis had been badly hurt by his opposition to the death penalty, an issue technically unrelated to race but, as the Horton ads had shown, bound up in white Americans' perceptions of "black criminality." Once the death penalty was reinstituted in Arkansas, Clinton as governor supported it, even to the point of allowing execution of a severely brain-damaged convicted killer (who happened to be black) in early 1992.[37] More significantly, Clinton made a point of symbolically distancing his campaign from Jesse Jackson, the most visible spokesman for the black community and a lightning rod for white hostility. By May of 1992, the two had already had one public spat, but a real fight broke out in mid-June when Clinton spoke at a meeting of the "Rainbow Coalition." The previous evening, Jackson's "leadership conference" had featured an appearance by rap singer Lisa Williamson ("Sister Souljah"). A month earlier, after the Los Angeles riots, Williamson had seemed to defend the assaults by black youths on innocent white bystanders. "I mean if black people kill black people every day, why not have a week and kill white people?" she had told a Washington *Post* reporter.[38] While a stunned Jesse Jackson fumed silently, the likely Democratic nominee scolded him and the conference organizers for giving Williamson a forum. The "kind of hatred" she had shown did no honor to the goals of the Rainbow Coalition, Clinton lectured. "If you took the words 'white' and 'black' and reversed them, you might think David Duke was giving that speech."[39]

Jackson, already miffed by Clinton's decision to exclude him from the list of potential vice-presidential candidates, declared that the episode proved that Clinton had a "character flaw." Knowing that he had strong support from other black political leaders, the Arkansas governor gambled that any drop-off in black turnout would be more than offset by support picked up among whites. And he was right. African American voters (who traditionally voted Democratic) dropped from 10 percent of

37. Allen and Portis, *Comeback Kid,* 182–85.
38. Washington *Post,* May 13, 1992.
39. Washington *Post,* May 14, 1992.

the 1988 electorate to 8 percent in 1992, but the loss was more than offset by Democratic increases, particularly among white southern voters for whom Jackson was anathema.[40] And outside the South, Clinton's move captured the admiration of many of the Reagan Democrats. As a white North Philadelphia electrician told two journalists covering the campaign, "The day he told off that fucking Jackson is the day he got my vote."[41]

In the end, Clinton's victory was made possible by a number of factors, none more important than George Bush's inability to shape a message that reassured the economic fears of voters. Almost all polls showed that the majority of voters cast their ballots *against* George Bush as much or more than *for* the specific policies of Bill Clinton.

But the most significant legacy of the campaign may have been the emergence, withdrawal, and reemergence of independent candidate Ross Perot. Perot proved unlike any previous third-party presidential contender. He wrapped equal parts of self-confidence, naïveté, paranoia, and political shrewdness into a folksy west Texas persona. Although the billionaire had built much of his fortune by pulling insider deals with federal and state government, he proved a master at promoting himself as the ultimate "can-do outsider" who—when questioned about the intractable problems of governing—insisted that it was just a simple matter of "cleaning out the barn" or "looking under the hood."

Perot released a campaign book filled with bar graphs and "issue positions" and flooded the airwaves with unprecedented half-hour political "infomercials." Promising to assemble experts who would somehow miraculously devise solutions, and offering a few glib generalizations and breathtaking promises ("We can balance the budget without breaking a sweat"), Perot avoided taking a stand on every substantive issue. In fact, beyond simplistic homilies and a commitment to reducing the national deficit, his was virtually a content-free campaign. And yet, at one point, four of every ten voters supported the Texas businessman, and 19 percent of the electorate ultimately cast their ballots for him.[42]

The willingness of millions to embrace a free-floating candidate like

40. New York *Times,* November 5, 1992.
41. Germond and Witcover, *Mad as Hell,* 305.
42. Ceaser and Busch, *Upside Down and Inside Out,* 90.

Perot suggests the emergence of a large minority within the electorate only marginally committed to either of the two political parties or even to a coherent political philosophy. Bill Clinton's narrow victory gave him almost no leverage. With no real mandate, but a commitment to dealing with such intractable issues as the need for universal health-care coverage, welfare and campaign-financing reform, and deficit reduction, the Democratic president had little room to maneuver. And when he next went to the voters, he would be the incumbent on the defensive, not the outsider on the attack.

Given Clinton's precarious election, his first two years in office were not without achievement. Abroad, national policy makers grappled with continuing trouble spots from the former Yugoslavia to the Horn of Africa, but there were reasons for hope: the peaceful transfer of power to a majority black government in South Africa, the accelerating peace process between Arabs and Israelis in the Middle East, even the astonishing prospect of serious negotiations to end Ireland's centuries-old blood feud. The collapse of international Communism had removed the greatest threat to national security and dramatically reduced the likelihood of nuclear conflict.

In dealing with domestic politics, Clinton's style seemed more akin to that of the hero in *The Perils of Pauline* than to that of a thoughtful administrator, but he rescued the North American Free Trade Agreement with a last-minute blitz of lobbying, he pushed through a wide-ranging crime bill, and—most significantly—he made substantial progress in reducing the budget-busting deficits that had exploded during the Reagan-Bush years. At the same time, the general economic indices reflected continued growth in economic investment, improvements in productivity, and a steady (if unspectacular) pattern of expansion and job growth, all without significant increases in inflation.

Such successes seemed more than balanced, however, by repeated political missteps, which began during Clinton's first days in office. He frustrated supporters and enraged conservative opponents by initially supporting gay rights in the armed forces, then backing down in the face of opposition from military leaders and their Capitol Hill allies. Over the next two years he stumbled on campaign and welfare reform, and the centerpiece of his domestic policy—universal health care—went down to ignominious defeat. Journalists depicted an administration overwhelmed by chaotic decision making within the White House and a tendency to compromise at the first hint of resistance. And American voters were less impressed by unspectacular overall improvements in the economy than by the constant headlines describing the downsizing of major corporations, the decline of high-paying blue-collar jobs, and the rise of low-paying service-sector employment.

As the by-elections of 1994 approached, with large numbers of Democratic incumbents up for election at the state and national levels, the Clinton-led Democratic Party braced for a Republican resurgency. But only a handful of GOP true believers anticipated their good fortune. The Democratic Party seemed to implode as voters administered one of the most devastating defeats ever suffered by an incumbent political party in an off-year election. With a gain of fifty-one seats, Republicans took control of the House of Representatives for the first time in forty years. In the Senate, every Republican incumbent won easily, but Democrats lost eight seats, and—with the party switch of Alabama's Richard Shelby— the GOP enjoyed a comfortable majority.

More than half of the Democratic losses came in the South. Beginning with the passage of the Civil Rights Act of 1964, white southern voters had increasingly supported Republican presidential candidates. In their 1987 study of southern politics, Earl and Merle Black argued that the general conservatism of Republican presidential candidates was a much closer match for the interests and beliefs of the South's growing white middle class. Between 1964 and 1988, the percentage of white southerners who voted for Republican presidential candidates grew from less than 50 percent to approximately 70 percent. Although Democrats continued to control state and local offices, their base steadily eroded throughout the 1980s as increasing numbers of white middle-class (and many low-income white) voters abandoned the Democratic Party and voted for GOP candidates at all levels.[43]

Political observers, particularly moderate to conservative Democrats,

43. Earl Black and Merle Black, *Politics and Society in the South* (Cambridge, Mass.: Harvard University Press, 1987), 213–76; Earl Black and Merle Black, *The Vital South: How Presidents Are Elected* (Cambridge, Mass.: Harvard University Press, 1992), 295.

attributed part of the GOP upsurge—especially among southern House Republicans—to two related developments: reapportionment and redistricting. The census of 1990 reflected a population shift to the suburbs, the heartland of southern Republicanism. In the reapportionment battles that followed, the suburbs gained new strength, while the creation of a number of safely "black" districts siphoned off African American voters and left "moderate" and conservative white Democrats vulnerable to Republican challenges.

The evidence is by no means clear that the creation of majority black districts played a significant role in southern GOP gains in 1994. In any case, Republican victories stretched across the whole country. White voters who two years earlier had divided almost equally between Bill Clinton and George Bush went for the GOP by three to two; among white males the edge was even greater. Self-described "independents" apportioned their 1992 ballots almost equally among Clinton, Bush, and Ross Perot; in 1994 two-thirds of those Perot voters went Republican.[44]

American political movements (or political parties) are seldom built on single causes or coherent ideologies. Nevertheless, conventional wisdom held that the one comprehensive issue that drove this electoral upheaval was middle-class voters' rejection of the president and his "big-government" policies in a desire to resume the Reagan revolution begun in 1980. If so, it seemed an odd response to changes sweeping the American economy.

During the twelve years of the Reagan-Bush administrations, the median wage earner in the United States saw his or her income decline 5 percent in real dollars after adjustments for inflation. During the same years, taxpayers in the top 5 percent saw their income increase nearly 30 percent, while the top 1 percent fared even better: their earnings rose 78 percent.[45] By the time of the 1994 election, the top 20 percent of American households received 55 percent of *after-tax* income and owned 85 percent

44. New York *Times,* November 10, 1994.
45. John Cassidy, "Who Killed the Middle Class?" *New Yorker,* October 16, 1995, p. 113. Ironically, Kevin Phillips, one of the most influential Republican strategists of the 1960s and 1970s, became the most unsparing critic of the economic consequences of the Republican revolution in his book *The Politics of Rich and Poor: Wealth and the American Electorate in the Reagan Aftermath* (New York: Random House, 1990).

of the country's marketable wealth. And the closer to the top of the income pyramid, the greater the increases. Between 1983 and 1994, the national net worth rose $6.5 trillion dollars; the top one-half of 1 percent of America's population received more than half of that gain. By the mid-1990s, the top 1 percent of Americans controlled over 40 percent of the nation's wealth, an imbalance in national income and resources not seen since the 1930s.[46]

And the trend toward increasing inequality continued even as productivity and business profits soared through the early 1990s.[47] International economists have noted a similar pattern in much of the Western industrial world, particularly in Great Britain. But the shifts elsewhere measured far less than those in the United States—which has long prided itself on being an egalitarian society. It is sometimes difficult to measure long-term trends in economic change; the public seems far more predisposed to accept news that reinforces their sense of unease and insecurity. When journalist John Cassidy surveyed the much-feared phenomenon of "downsizing" as it had manifested itself in the 1970s, 1980s, and early 1990s, he found that most economists—liberal and conservative—believed that the media had exaggerated the long-term job instability of skilled workers and middle-level managers. But even in this rosier picture of the transformation of the American economy, Cassidy found that the costs of economic change were "still being borne primarily by the poor and ill-educated." In any case, one fundamental change in the American economy seemed indisputable: as the twentieth century drew toward a close, this country was well on its way to becoming one of the most economically stratified industrial nations in the developed world.[48]

By the mid-1990s, all but the most ideologically committed economists

46. New York *Times,* April 17, 1995; Paul Krugman, "What the Public Doesn't Know Can't Hurt Us," *Washington Monthly,* October, 1995, p. 8.

47. New York *Times,* August 14, 1995.

48. Gary Burtless, Richard Freeman, and Robert Solow, *Widening Earnings Inequality* (Washington, D.C.: Urban Institute, 1994); Steve Nickell and Brian Bell, "The Collapse in Demand for the Unskilled," *Oxford Review of Economic Policy,* Spring, 1995; John Cassidy, "All Worked Up," *New Yorker,* April 22, 1996, p. 54. For evidence of the growing pay divide between rich and poor in Great Britain, see the highlights of the British government's 1995 *New Earnings Survey* published in the *Times* of London, September 29, 1995.

had concluded that underlying structural elements were the main cause of these changes. The internationalization of trade, the opening of a global labor economy, the decline of trade unions, and the displacement of semi-skilled and skilled workers through new technologies have been the key factors in shifting income to the wealthy and the upper-middle class. The result has been a decline in the economic well-being of working-class and lower-middle-class Americans, creating a growing underclass and plunging millions of children into poverty. No magic wand can restore America to universally rising incomes and widespread economic security.[49]

But if the conservative tax and spending policies of the 1980s and early 1990s were secondary factors in the shift of income from poor to rich, they clearly played a contributory role. From the standpoint of self-interest, it is understandable why affluent Americans—those at the top 20 percent of the income scale—should endorse a return to the 1980s. They had never had it so good. And yet much of the hostility toward the "welfare state" came from middle-class voters who continued to see the dependent and "deviant" as the cause of their growing insecurity.

On the eve of the 1994 election, political analyst William Schneider argued there was a fundamental link between this antifederal upsurge and the emergence of a politically dominant suburban America. Suburbanization, argued Schneider, inevitably reinforced the "privatization of American life and culture." Middle- and upper-income families were able to escape the increasingly unruly public spaces of decaying central cities by creating a "secure and controlled environment" in malls and private automobiles (as opposed to public transportation). The advent of cable television and video rentals even ensured private entertainment space within their homes.[50]

49. Cassidy, "Who Killed the Middle Class?" 121. Even when observers agree that these factors have threatened the well-being of America's working and middle classes, they do not agree on solutions. Robert Reich, in *The Work of Nations: Preparing Ourselves for Twenty-first-Century Capitalism* (New York: Alfred A. Knopf, 1991), 196–221, insists that there is no escape from the arena of international trade; he proposes massive upgrading of job skills for those Americans most jeopardized by low-wage international competition. Edward N. Luttwak, *The Endangered American Dream* (New York: Simon & Schuster, 1993), 153–81, supports much more nationalistic policies.

50. William Schneider, "The Suburban Century Begins," *Atlantic Monthly*, July, 1992, p. 37.

Isolated from the escalating demands of the growing urban underclass, residents of America's suburbs could control their own local government, and they could buy good schools and safe streets (or at least better schools and safer streets than the inner city). To be sure, not all middle-class Americans, suburban or otherwise, were able to protect themselves from the vicissitudes of the new economic order: the lack of job security and slowly falling incomes. "Big" government—the federal government— spent *their* hard-earned taxes for programs that, most suburbanites had concluded, were wasteful and inefficient and did nothing to help them. It was this critical group of swing voters to whom conservative Republicans appealed when they unveiled their platform for the 1994 campaign: the "Contract with America." Newly elected House minority leader Newt Gingrich promised a vote within 100 days on a combination of sweeping tax cuts and spending reductions that would shift government fiscal and social policy from "liberal" to "conservative" policies.[51] "Newt grasped the essential cultural revolt [of the 1980s and 1990s]," said one Republican strategist. "Middle-class people are not against rich people—they're against funding poor people."[52]

On close scrutiny, the Contract seemed less focused on ending the welfare state than on transferring its benefits from the undeserving poor to the deserving middle- and upper-income classes. For wealthy and upper-middle-class voters there was the promise of a 50 percent cut in the capital gains tax; for middle-class families, a $500-per-child tax credit, a repeal of

---

51. The "Contract" also proposed a number of cosmetic reforms aimed at streamlining the House, cutting its staff, and conducting a "comprehensive audit of Congress for waste, fraud or abuse." In addition, Republicans pledged to bring to a vote such longtime conservative goals as a presidential line-item veto and a "Balanced Budget" amendment to the Constitution. The only suggestions of sharply increased expenditures were in national defense: Republican House leaders demanded construction of an updated version of Ronald Reagan's old "Star Wars" missile-defense system and warned that "significant increases in defense funding may be necessary in the future." Perhaps mindful of the backlash against the 1992 Republican convention, Gingrich downplayed noneconomic issues that had formed the core of the religious right's agenda: abortion, prayer in the schools, and the restoration of "morality" in public life. See " 'Contract with America': House GOP Offers Descriptions of Bills to Enact Contract," *Congressional Quarterly,* November 19, 1994, p. 3375.

52. Connie Bruck, "Profile: The Politics of Perception," *New Yorker,* October 9, 1995, p. 62.

the federal income tax "marriage penalty," and additional tax credits for caring for elderly dependents. Social Security and Medicare, promised the Contract with America, were exempt from reductions. Indeed, for affluent older Americans there was the promise of a repeal of the 1993 tax increases on Social Security, an increase in the Social Security earnings limits, and tax incentives for private long-term-care insurance.[53]

Once in power, the new Republican majority abandoned some of its earlier commitments. Medicare, it turned out, was not so sacrosanct after all. But their election-year contract with the voters did reflect the priorities of this new majority. According to an analysis by the Treasury Department's Office of Tax Policy, the Senate and House tax measures introduced in 1995 by the new Republican majority gave more than 46 percent of the tax cuts to taxpayers earning more than $100,000 a year. Those earning less than $30,000 got 1 percent of the benefits, while the working poor on incomes of less than $10,000 were slated for a tax *increase* through reduction of the Earned Income Tax Credit.[54]

The Contract with America—even when measured against the hyperbole of most political platforms—amounted to little more than economic glossolalia. Congressman Gingrich and his fellow Republicans assured voters that any budget they introduced would include enough cuts to "ensure that the Federal budget deficit will be *less* than it would have been without the enactment of these [tax and spending] bills." But passage of only one plank—the $500-per-child tax credit—would decrease income tax receipts by approximately $20 billion a year. Budget analysts disagreed on the price tag in lost revenues that the other half-dozen proposed tax benefits would carry. Nor was any clear estimate given as to the cost of the GOP's vague proposals for a military buildup and the restoration of a

53. New York *Times,* December 11, 1994. Needless to say, the document made no mention of the $70 billion a year homeowners deducted from their taxes for mortgage interest and property taxes. (Simply by limiting the deductability of mortgage debt to $300,000—a measure that would affect less than 1 percent of the nation's taxpayers—the treasury would recoup $4 billion a year.) Nor was there any discussion of the oil, gas, and mining tax subsidies ($2 billion a year) or agricultural subsidies ($13–$16 billion annually, half going to agribusiness operations and farmers earning more than $100,000 a year). Dan Goodgame, "Reining in the Rich," *Time,* December 19, 1994, p. 24.

54. *Washington Monthly,* December, 1995, p. 3.

limited version of Ronald Reagan's old "Star Wars" missile-defense system. After some "best-guess" calculations, however, one public-policy analyst put the total cost of the GOP's wish list at a bare-bones minimum of $150–200 billion a year. Using the Contract's most optimistic projections, savings in welfare programs (the only substantial cutbacks proposed in the document) would amount to less than $8 billion a year. With Social Security, Medicare, and defense supposedly exempt from the budget knife, lawmakers would have to cut every other federal program by more than 40 percent.[55]

Of course, the Contract with America was unlikely to be adopted intact. Like most political platforms, it revealed far less about fiscal policy than about ideology and political strategy. Although the 1994 exit polls suggested a negative voter response to Democratic "big government," there was little evidence that the proposed capital gains tax cut galvanized many among the 39 percent of the potential voters who actually went to the polls. Apart from a vague support for fiscal conservatism and a generalized hostility toward President Clinton, the only item on the Republican agenda that seemed to strike an emotional chord among voters was the call for welfare reform.

Welfare reform was hardly a new issue. For more than two decades both parties had lamented the escalation of welfare costs. Of the campaign issues tested on focus groups by Bush in 1992, only the promise of welfare cuts provoked a strong positive response.[56] Early in his own campaign, Clinton, too, had laid out his plans for "ending welfare as we know it," proposing an ambitious program of job training and child support—coupled with provisions for continuing health-care coverage—to move able-bodied recipients into the work force. Once Clinton was in office, however, welfare reform took a back seat to his ill-fated health-care legislation.

But Gingrich's Contract with America offered something quite different from the programs suggested by Clinton or Bush. Indeed, it was a generation away in time and tone from earlier Republican proposals. Richard Nixon, after all, had once endorsed a guaranteed minimum income in an effort to encourage individuals to leave welfare and enter the

55. Michael Kramer, "Newt's Believe It or Not," *Time,* December 19, 1994, p. 44.
56. Kolbert, "Test-Marketing a President," 20.

job force. Reagan had promised voters that he would make welfare more efficient and less prone to abuse, but he had also assured them that he had no intention of destroying the nation's "safety net."

Gingrich and his fellow GOP House members began by calling for the end of the "entitlement status" of AFDC, Supplemental Security Income, public housing, and all nutritional programs (including food stamps, the Women, Infants and Children Nutritional Program, and the school lunch program). In fact, the idea was to abolish these programs on a federal level. The 1994 congressional appropriations—minus 10 to 20 percent— would be returned to the states in block grants. States could use the federal grants for such purposes as operating homes for unwed mothers, promoting adoptions, or constructing orphanages. But they would be explicitly barred from giving cash payments to teenaged mothers who gave birth to illegitimate children. Moreover, at the end of two years, teenaged mothers and their illegitimate children already on the welfare rolls would be ineligible for relief. In addition, states would have the option of terminating public assistance to any other individuals after two years, regardless of need. And after a combined total of five years on welfare, *all* recipients—regardless of circumstances—would be barred from receiving federally funded relief.[57]

It is not at all clear that most Americans approved the welfare policies advocated by the Contract with America. Although voters in both parties favored, in general terms, an "overhaul" of the welfare system, public attitudes toward the issue depended almost entirely on how pollsters phrased the questions. A slight majority of Americans believed that assistance to the poor should be reduced, but less than 40 percent of those who responded supported the GOP proposal to cut off welfare after two years, and 70 percent were willing to spend *more* money in the short run in order to train and prepare welfare recipients for employment.[58]

57. "'Contract with America,'" 3366–79; New York *Times,* December 9, 1994.

58. *Time*/CNN poll conducted by Yankelovich and Associates a month after the election, *Time,* December 19, 1994, p. 32. One postelection poll conducted by the New York *Times* showed that 75 percent of the American people professed complete ignorance of the "Contract with America," and when the specifics of Clinton's welfare proposals were compared with the Republicans', voters favored the president's plans two to one. New York *Times,* December 18, 1994.

Beleaguered defenders of the existing system retreated to their last line of defense: a call to protect the nation's children. And they had powerful arguments on their side. In 1995 the Luxembourg Group, an international social-science research consortium based in Europe, completed a comprehensive survey comparing child welfare among the thirteen most advanced European industrial democracies and the United States, Australia, Israel, and Canada. America's children ranked fifteenth, just ahead of those in Israel and Ireland. Had the research design included such in-kind benefits as child-care services and free health care, the United States would have ranked at the bottom.[59]

But Gingrich and his fellow conservatives argued that federal programs begun in the 1960s had failed. The elimination of welfare as a federal entitlement, they argued, would break the cycle of welfare dependency and restore individual "initiative and dignity" to its recipients. When confronted with the uncomfortable fact that the greatest impact of these cuts would be upon minorities, Gingrich brushed aside suggestions that the GOP's hostility to federal welfare was racist. And on one level he was certainly correct. Class fears and moral outrage played a critical role in demonizing welfare mothers; the hostility of middle- and upper-income taxpayers toward welfare recipients was far more complicated than a dressed-up version of the old southern demagogue's cry of "nigger, nigger, nigger."

But surely it was not simply a coincidence that the issue that resonated most powerfully during the 1994 political ad wars was the call for ending welfare (or that the second-most-emotional issue of the campaign was the growing anger over furnishing public assistance to Hispanic aliens).[60] Although whites, by a narrow margin, still constituted the majority of those individuals on the nation's welfare rolls, almost every American knew that, statistically, African Americans were far more likely to end up "on welfare." Almost every American knew that, statistically, the rate of illegiti-

59. New York *Times,* August 14, 1995.

60. Besides slashing public assistance to poor Americans and to aliens (including those legally in the United States), the only other proposals for cuts came in promises to eliminate the "social spending" from the Clinton administration's 1994 crime bill, a term Republican lawmakers had repeatedly used to characterize crime-prevention and rehabilitation programs.

macy and welfare dependency was higher in the African American community than among whites. As one longtime student of welfare reform observed, Republicans were exploiting the anger of middle-class taxpayers who believed that their tax dollars were going to the undeserving poor, particularly "young women, without education, who are long-term dependents and whose dependency is passed on from generation to generation." The unspoken subtext of this outlook was the belief that "these women are inner-city substance-abusing blacks spawning a criminal class."[61]

The issue resonated with a critical minority of swing voters because it sat squarely in the middle of a changed dialogue on the respective roles played by nature and nurture in shaping the politics of race in America. For much of the twentieth century, American liberals had tended to emphasize the environmental factors that shaped antisocial behavior, while conservatives resisted the notion that "immoral" choices and antisocial behavior flowed only from economic deprivation. Since the 1930s—certainly since the 1960s—the argument has been over the balance between individual responsibility and the obligation of a society to furnish *opportunities* for those who begin life handicapped by social, economic, and cultural disadvantages.

Just two weeks before the smashing Republican victory of 1994, however, the *New York Times Magazine* heralded the publication of a controversial new book, *The Bell Curve: Intelligence and Class Structure in American Life,* by Richard Herrnstein and Charles Murray. There was a singular aptness in the publication of *The Bell Curve* on the eve of the 1994 election, for like the election itself, the book reflected a deep shift in the assumptions that underlay the thinking of Americans on the emotional subjects of race and public policy.[62]

Ten years earlier, Charles Murray had previewed his ideas in *Losing Ground,* a study of national welfare policy (or "social policy," as he preferred to call it). Funded by the Manhattan Institute, one of the new conservative think tanks that sprang up in the Reagan years, the book

61. New York *Times,* November 16, 1994.
62. Richard Herrnstein and Charles Murray, *The Bell Curve: Intelligence and Class Structure in American Life* (New York: Free Press, 1994).

reflected the conventional wisdom of Republican conservatism in the 1980s: *i.e.,* that Lyndon Johnson's War on Poverty had been far more successful at wasting the taxpayers' money than at ending poverty.

But Murray's message went on to indict the very notion of government welfare, and he insisted that federally funded welfare programs inevitably rewarded the "least law-abiding," the "least capable," and the "least responsible" among the poor. The result (for Murray, at least) was clear: the encouragement of socially undesirable activities by America's underclass. Strapping young men refused to take responsibility for their illegal offspring or to accept entry-level jobs, and teenage girls had illegitimate babies to collect welfare payments. The only hope for a declining America was to scrap the "entire federal welfare and income-support structure for working-aged persons, including AFDC, Medicaid, Food Stamps, Unemployment Insurance, Worker's Compensation, subsidized housing, disability insurance, and the rest."[63] Some softhearted Americans—even those who saw themselves as conservatives—might flinch from such a draconian solution, admitted Murray, but he warned against sentimentality. Abandoning such wasteful programs would mean that the "lives of large numbers of poor people would be radically changed for the better" by creating a setting in which hard work was rewarded and slothfulness punished. The real barrier to change, argued Murray, was "not the pain it would cause the intended beneficiaries of the present system, but the pain it would cause the donors."[64]

In some respects, the most intriguing aspect of *Losing Ground* lay in the issues that Murray did not confront. He acknowledged that black Americans—even in the North, where official, legal discrimination had long since ceased to exist—fared badly when compared with whites. Since he opposed affirmative-action programs and argued that racial discrimination was an insignificant factor in explaining the poor social and economic status of blacks, his findings seemed to suggest that blacks had failed disproportionately because of their own limitations. But beyond suggesting that black poverty and poor "performance" were the products

---

63. Charles Murray, *Losing Ground: American Social Policy, 1950–1980* (New York: Basic Books, 1984), 227–28.
64. *Ibid.,* 229, 236.

of internal cultural deficiencies (the "young ghetto black on his way up was not cheered on his way, as the young Jewish or Chinese . . . youth has been") or destructive welfare policies ("social policy [in the 1960s] actively pressed on the ghetto: 'It's not your fault'"), Murray seemed to shy away from the racial implications of his argument.[65]

With the publication of *The Bell Curve,* the issue of race as it had surfaced in American politics with George Wallace's forays north had come full circle. Herrnstein, Murray's coauthor (who died just weeks before the book was published), had spent much of his professional career arguing that twentieth-century liberal ideologues had conspired to conceal the uncomfortable reality that genetically inherent IQ limited the capabilities of some racial (and ethnic) groups. To put it more bluntly, a racial hierarchy of intelligence existed, with East Asians at the top (along with Ashkenazi Jews), most American "whites" just below, Hispanics farther down the scale, and blacks at the absolute bottom. Herrnstein's argument was not racist in the traditional sense; he did not argue that all blacks were inferior to all whites. In fact, he concluded that about 10 percent of whites were also doomed to failure by low intelligence. But people of color were the real threat to American society.[66]

The Bell Curve made token references to the problems welfare dependency created for the deserving poor, and its authors spoke disdainfully of the "chilling implications of social Darwinism." But their analysis and prescriptions bore far more similarities to than differences from the work of such nineteenth-century social Darwinists as Herbert Spencer and William Graham Sumner.[67] To help the poor or disadvantaged was a fool's errand. Under the iron influence of genetic determinism, the intelligent

65. *Ibid.,* 191.

66. Herrnstein and Murray argued that a decline in the "self-selection" process meant that the earlier generation of immigrants ("brave, hard-working, imaginative, self-starting—and probably smart") had been replaced by sluggards for whom "immigrating to America can be . . . a much easier option than staying where he is." The only hope of remedying this problem, they suggested, was to discourage low-IQ immigrants, such as Hispanics and Haitians, and to encourage those from high-IQ gene pools, such as Asians. Herrnstein and Murray, *Bell Curve,* 360, 549.

67. Richard Hofstadter, *Social Darwinism in American Thought* (Boston: Beacon Press, 1959), 41, 56.

would rise to the top in the new meritocracy created by the information revolution, and the intellectually stunted would retreat into squalor, criminality, and (in the case of women) the reproduction of illegitimate, low-IQ offspring.

Any advantages gained by improving the environmental setting of the "cognitively disadvantaged" would be so limited and the costs so great that almost every conceivable antipoverty program would fail when costs were weighed against benefits to the individuals involved and to the larger society. Although the two authors made a halfhearted attempt to suggest what they called "A Place for Everyone" in American society, they reached irremediably bleak conclusions. In apocalyptic tones they described the "Coming of the Custodial State" in which the cognitively privileged middle and upper classes would ultimately create a "high tech and more lavish version of the Indian reservation" to contain and control a rapidly breeding criminal underclass.[68]

In 1963, before he mastered the use of coded language, George Wallace bluntly expressed his view that blacks were *inherently* lazy, lacking in intelligence, sexually promiscuous, and prone to commit the most "atrocious acts of humanity, such as rape, assault and murder."[69] Today, cruder forms of racism remain the province of marginal white-supremacy groups such as the Aryan Nation, or of African American demagogues like Louis Farrakhan, whose fulminations against Jewish "bloodsuckers" and "white devils" seem designed to prove that bigotry is an equal opportunity employer.[70] Herrnstein and Murray's sober, even regretful, tone seemed to distance their conclusions from Wallace's vulgar racism, but *The Bell Curve*—despite the elaborate statistical tables, footnotes, and appendices—was simply the latest version of a centuries-old argument justifying white supremacy and black subordination.

Although Herrnstein and Murray's scholarly presentation intimidated many readers (and reviewers), the fundamental inconsistencies in the book should have been obvious. In one of the most devastating critiques, Ste-

68. Herrnstein and Murray, *Bell Curve,* 526.
69. Art Wallace to George Wallace, August 13, 1963, George Wallace to Art Wallace, September 13, 1963, both in "Segregation File," Drawer 399, George Wallace Papers, Alabama Department of Archives and History.
70. London *Times,* October 15, 16, 1995.

phen Jay Gould, author of *The Mismeasure of Man,* dismantled much of *The Bell Curve*'s psychometric and statistical foundation. At best, he charged, the authors were disingenuous; at worst, downright dishonest in their misuse of statistics, their omission of evidence contradicting their point of view, and their relentless subordination of evidence to ideology. The book was not a work of social theory or population genetics at all, concluded Gould, but a "manifesto of conservative ideology."[71] Another reviewer acidly observed, "*The Bell Curve* is not only sleazy; it is, intellectually, a mess."[72]

Such attacks seemed only to validate the significance of the Herrnstein-Murray book. *Losing Ground* had been greeted with disdain by most mainstream reviewers in 1984; *The Bell Curve* quickly climbed toward the top of the New York *Times* best-seller list. Murray became a regular on radio and television talk shows, glibly explaining the results of his study of nature and nurture. Although he assumed the tone of a reluctant bearer of bad news and professed concern over the possibility that his findings might be used by racists, he always went on, as one critic pointed out, to "say that their findings only reflect what people already think in their heart of hearts—which is, that blacks and white trash are born irremediably dumb, that black Americans have been overpromoted in the academy, that smarter white workers have been displaced by incompetent black ones at the behest of the federal government."[73]

The New York *Times*—the newspaper of record in the United States—assigned science reporter Malcolm Browne to review *The Bell Curve*. It was one of the longest reviews published by the *Times* during 1994. And despite a few quibbles over the interpretation of evidence, Browne concluded that the authors had made a "strong case that America's population is becoming dangerously polarized between a smart, rich, educated elite and a population of unintelligent, poor and uneducated people." The time was approaching, suggested the reviewer, when society had the "right—perhaps even the duty—to strengthen our species' cognitive

71. Stephen Jay Gould, "Curveball," *New Yorker,* November 28, 1994, pp. 139–40.

72. Alan Ryan, "Apocalypse Now?" *New York Review of Books,* November 17, 1994, p. 11.

73. Ryan, "Apocalypse Now?" 8.

defenses against an increasingly dangerous global environment." Stripped of doublespeak, the science reporter for the New York *Times* was suggesting that America's survival depended upon the acceptance of low IQ as a "disease" that should be "treated" through genetic manipulation and/or the embrace of eugenics as a national policy.[74]

Geoffrey Cowley, writing in *Newsweek,* was even more explicit in defending the racial implications of *The Bell Curve.* The authors' study was based upon work that was "overwhelmingly mainstream," asserted Cowley. (In fact, much of the research on which Herrnstein and Murray relied was financed by the Pioneer Fund, a New York–based research organization founded in 1937 by two American scientists who had supported Hitler's eugenics policies. Financial support for the organization came from Wickliffe Draper, a wealthy textile manufacturer turned eugenicist who had also flirted with Nazism and advocated the "repatriation" of "genetically inferior" blacks to Africa as late as the mid-1950s.) Intelligence, Cowley said, in quoting one researcher, was primarily a matter of genetics; so long as the environment was "adequate," it had little or no impact on the achievement level of individuals. Social scientists had long agreed, Cowley added, that the gap between black and white intelligence involved "genetic as well as environmental factors." But he suggested that as much as 70 percent of IQ differences stemmed from genetic inheritance. If Herrnstein and Murray had failed to convince all their readers, they had nevertheless found a receptive audience for their argument that the wretched condition of a large percentage of African Americans had little to do with historical racism or long-term cultural and economic deprivation because poverty, criminality, and welfare dependency were directly linked with racially determined—and relatively fixed—low IQs.[75]

74. Malcolm Browne, "What Is Intelligence and Who Has It?" *New York Times Book Review,* October 16, 1994, pp. 3, 41, 45. The response to *The Bell Curve,* it should be noted, did not precisely follow traditional "liberal-conservative" fault lines. Along with the expected attacks from such liberal stalwarts as the *Nation,* the *New Yorker,* the *Progressive,* and the *New York Review of Books,* there was a blistering review from the *Wall Street Journal.* Clearly, however, the once-unthinkable had become part of the public debate over race and politics.

75. Geoffrey Cowley, "Testing the Science of Intelligence," *Newsweek,* October 24, 1994, pp. 56–60. For the connection with the Pioneer Fund, see Lane, "The Tainted Sources of

But *The Bell Curve* seemed unlikely to become a manifesto for political activists. Murray's bleak analysis and gloomy warnings of inevitable conflict between the genetically capable and the incurably stupid ran counter to the optimistic "can-do" style adopted by most successful American politicians, conservative or liberal. And respectable racism—even dressed up with an elaborate scholarly apparatus—runs against the grain of a society that has emphasized the possibilities of all individuals. Most Americans are more comfortable with a set of ideas that Stanford historian George Frederickson has labeled "cultural essentialism."[76]

In his 1995 book *The End of Racism: Principles for a Multiracial Society,* conservative writer Dinesh D'Souza describes with crude generalizations a pattern of behavior among contemporary blacks that parallels nineteenth- and twentieth-century stereotypes about shiftless and oversexed "darkies." In emotive language, he depicts a black ghetto "culture" of hedonism, violence, and social irresponsibility, a culture in which young black men are twice as likely to be unemployed as their white counterparts, eight times as likely to die by homicide, and ten times as likely to be in prison, on parole, or on probation.[77] Like Herrnstein and Murray, D'Souza believes that the foolish generosity of the welfare state reinforces deviant behavior by protecting its recipients from the consequences of their antisocial actions. But he does not share the belief that inexorable genetic limitations doom blacks to a life in the ghetto. Nor does he believe that race prejudice remains a serious barrier to achievement by minorities. Members of the underclass are not victims of white racism or even of a crippling environment. They can choose to turn their backs on this willful pathology of depravity and antisocial behavior by embracing the conservative values of the dominant "white" culture.[78]

That racism is no longer an impenetrable barrier to success for African

'The Bell Curve,'" *New York Review of Books,* December 1, 1994, pp. 14–16, and Stefan Kuehl, *The Nazi Connection: Eugenics, American Racism, and German National Socialism* (New York: Oxford University Press, 1994), 5–14.

76. George M. Frederickson, "Demonizing the American Dilemma," *New York Review of Books,* October 19, 1995, p. 16.

77. London *Times,* October 15, 1995, p. 20.

78. Dinesh D'Souza, *The End of Racism: Principles for a Multiracial Society* (New York: Free Press, 1995).

Americans is hardly a new idea. Certainly, there is a retreat from the racial absolutism of the 1950s and 1960s and a growing tolerance among whites for blacks who share their conservative values. The black sociologist William Julius Wilson said something along this same line (albeit much more subtly) in 1978 in his book *The Declining Significance of Race*.[79] And retired general Colin Powell's enormous appeal to conservative (and moderate) white voters at the time of the publication of his 1995 autobiography reflects something of the changes in white attitudes over the last half-century. But there is hardly an "end to racism," as D'Souza boldly proclaims.

Deep shifts in political opinion do not turn on a single issue. Busing and the political liabilities of affirmative action were not the only reasons conservatives advanced toward a political majority during the Reagan years. Willie Horton ads did not sink Michael Dukakis' bid for the presidency in 1988, and the singling out of welfare recipients as scapegoats for the intractable problems of crime and social disorder are only part of the story of the landslide Republican victory of 1994. Looking backward over three decades, however, we can see the subtle shifts in the public rhetoric about race within the context of a more general debasement of the culture of American politics.

A steady escalation in the use of political invective has prevailed across the ideological spectrum, but liberals, operating in an increasingly conservative political climate, have generally come off second best against their conservative opponents. (The success of liberal pressure groups in sinking the nomination of Robert Bork to the United States Supreme Court by exaggerating and misrepresenting his views was a rare exception to the rule.) Those who would compromise, particularly those liberals who would compromise, operate from a distinct disadvantage. However often they try to depict their opponents as heartless plutocrats intent on throwing widows and orphans into the streets, their demons seldom match those of the radical right.

Only a week before the 1994 congressional elections, Newt Gingrich, the acknowledged political commander-in-chief of the emerging Republican majority, privately told a group of pro-GOP lobbyists that his cam-

---

79. William Julius Wilson, *The Declining Significance of Race: Blacks and Changing American Institutions* (Chicago: University of Chicago Press, 1978).

paign strategy was to depict Clinton Democrats as "the enemy of normal Americans" and as advocates of "Stalinist" measures.[80] Just thirty-six hours before election day, Gingrich referred to the tragic incident in South Carolina in which a young mother—ostensibly a devout, born-again Christian—had drowned her two children. Her action "vividly reminds every American how sick their society is getting and how much we have to have change." And the "only way you get change is to vote Republican."[81]

Throughout the 1980s, Gingrich had worked to convince frustrated members of his party that their only hope for political victory was to reshape the traditional give-and-take of American politics into a "battleground" between godly Republicans and the "secular anti-religious view of the left" which shaped the Democratic Party.[82] In the spring of 1988, he told a *Wall Street Journal* reporter that Democrats were not simply politically misguided: "These people are sick."[83] As one of his Republican colleagues said with a combination of admiration and apprehension, Gingrich had come to believe that the politics of *perception* was everything. It did not matter what really happened, said Michael Johnson; the House Republican leader passionately believed that "if you can describe it your way, *you* define it."[84]

And what was this world of perception? "He means to create a Manichaean scheme in domestic politics as severe and confrontational as the struggle with Soviet Communism at the height of the Cold War," concluded *New Yorker* journalist and essayist David Remnick. Thus, Gingrich distributed to his followers a word list to be used to define Democrats: *sick, traitors, corrupt, bizarre, cheat, steal, devour, self-serving,* and *criminal rights.* In the GOP leader's political universe there would be "no mercy for the 'other side' or for anyone else." As longtime conservative fundraiser Paul Weyrich said admiringly, "Newt Gingrich is the first conservative I have ever known who knows how to use power."[85]

80. New York *Times,* November 10, 1994.

81. Atlanta *Journal-Constitution,* November 7, 1994.

82. New York *Times,* November 16, 1994.

83. *Wall Street Journal,* May 10, 1988.

84. Bruck, "Profile: The Politics of Perception," 59.

85. David Remnick, "Lost in Space," *New Yorker,* December 5, 1994, p. 86; Bruck, "Profile: The Politics of Perception," 62, 70. That same invective could be (and was) applied

The shift in the tone of political rhetoric mirrored that in the larger culture. America's media—mainstream and tabloid—found that they could capture the attention of readers and viewers only by increasing the level of hyperbole, sensationalism, and cynicism until—in one critic's words—"even an issue of *Good Housekeeping* practically foams at the mouth."[86] In such a "culture of aggression," the press often seemed less "liberal" or "conservative" than intent on savaging more moderate or "compromising" individuals. In fact, George Wallace would probably come across as a mealymouthed moderate when juxtaposed with today's right-wing-radical talk-show hosts. Admittedly, much of the vitriol is *rhetoric.* And we should not exaggerate the elevated nature of American politics over the last two hundred years. Demons have often been at the core of our political campaigns, and levels of incivility inevitably rise during those periods when broad political consensus breaks down. Still, there has been a long tradition in which campaign hyperbole is set aside on the day after the election. The loser offers a tight-lipped smile and message of congratulation, and the winner generously acknowledges his former opponent's good intentions. But the take-no-prisoners political culture of the 1990s was captured in Newt Gingrich's press conference following the 1994 elections. Basking in the glow of the sweeping victory that would transform him from House minority leader to Speaker of the House, Gingrich sneered at the humbled Bill Clinton and his wife. They were "counterculture at Yale" and they remained so, he told reporters. "They really are left-wing elitists."[87]

Creating a bipolar political system of good and evil, right and wrong, inevitably invites higher levels of voter frustration and anger, for such imperatives place upon the political system impossible demands. Despite election-year promises, the welfare state will not wither away, and the public reassertion of "moral values" and the unleashing of "individual

---

against "moderate" conservatives who deviated from the orthodoxies of the new right, as Colin Powell and Sheila Burke (Republican Senate majority leader Robert Dole's chief-of-staff) discovered. New York *Times,* November 2, 1995; Jason DeParle, "Sheila Burke Is the Militant Feminist Commie Peacenik Who's Telling Bob Dole What to Think," *New York Times Magazine,* November 12, 1995, 32–38, 90, 100, 102, 104–105.

86. Adam Gopnik, "Read All About It," *New Yorker,* December 12, 1994, p. 93.

87. New York *Times,* November 10, 1994.

empowerment" through the "free enterprise system" will never succeed in restoring a lost moral Eden or a secure and stable economic society. A small number of Americans have retreated into violent and apocalyptic antipolitical movements. By mid-1996, there were more than 1,000 "patriot" groups and armed citizen militias across the nation. Although their ideological outlook covered a spectrum from outright racism to traditional conservatism, most shared paranoid conspiracy theories that saw the federal government as the instrument of a coming totalitarian "one-world" regime.[88]

For most Americans, however, the response seems closer to that of frustrated consumers than armed revolutionaries. In the spring of 1995 Newt Gingrich was hailed as the most important congressional figure in the twentieth century; six months later he was already suffering from the pendulum swing of the electorate's frustrations. In his 1992 book *Who Will Tell the People?* reporter William Greider suggested that voters had already concluded that election campaigns, "like television commercials," were far more a matter of entertainment than a matter of deep commitment. The emotional images on the screen gave voters an "imagined moment of aroused feeling—a transient emotional bond with those who will hold power, a chance to identify with certain idealized qualities, but not an opportunity to connect with real governing power." Thus we see the electorate off in search of Oz, chasing will-of-the-wisp candidates like billionaire Ross Perot, who offers little more than slogans and the promise of voter "empowerment" through the global village of television town meetings, or like magazine-publishing magnate Steve Forbes, who spends several million dollars of his $400 million fortune to peddle the virtues of a flat-tax system. Greider's observation may explain why younger voters, even more sophisticated and jaded than their elders, are dropping off the voting rolls in growing numbers.[89]

In such a political climate, political operatives unconcerned with any goal except winning face an irresistible temptation to reach deep into the rucksack of traditional racism. But much has changed in southern and

---

88. *USA Today/International Edition,* April 18, 1996, p. 5-A.

89. William Greider, *Who Will Tell the People? The Betrayal of American Democracy* (New York: Simon & Schuster, 1992), 278n4, 437.

American politics in the years since George Wallace promised his close friends in 1958 that he would "never be out-niggered again." Wallace himself quickly learned to adapt with the times. Over the next fifteen years, he showed how a politician—by using language that was not explicitly racial but was unmistakable in its symbolic intent—could have the best of both worlds. He could reap the benefits of some of the most reprehensible attitudes in our culture and innocently proclaim the purest of motives. Racism—though it continues as a subtext in American politics—no longer wears the rhetorical garments of earlier generations.

Still, the powerfully evocative images of a threatening black underclass reflect fears deeply lodged in our national historical memory. During his insurgent campaign of 1996, presidential aspirant Patrick Buchanan broke ranks with fellow Republicans by rejecting the link between unrestrained capitalism and the cultural conservatism of the new right—evidence of the increasing instability of the old coalition built upon social issues and right-wing economic policies. Despite his spirited attacks on multinational corporations, however, Buchanan's polemics were mainly a sideshow to his ongoing barrage against the more traditional enemies of the ultraright: homosexuals, abortionists, feminists, and Jews. And the old themes remained. It was Buchanan who angrily denounced the continuing flow of immigrants into the United States on the grounds that "they are not English-speaking white people from Western Europe, they are Spanish-speaking brown and black people from Mexico, Latin America and the Caribbean."[90] Even Newt Gingrich, who has carefully sought to insulate himself from charges of racism, is not above mobilizing the old fears. When he complains of inner-city "welfare Americans" who "quit their jobs" and "start cheating on the rent," who "start fighting on Saturday night" and "break up their family," he does not have to refer to skin color.[91]

Over the last century and a half, Americans have seen many of their demons slip away: the monstrous symbol of the slavocracy (and white southerners' counterimage of the equally monstrous northern abolition-

90. "The Beltway Populist," *Newsweek*, March 4, 1996, p. 26; London *Times*, February 22, 1996, p. 12.
91. Bruck, "Profile: The Politics of Perception," 62.

ist), the Church of Rome ("Whore of the Devil"), and in our own time, the evil empire of international Communism. In his subtle exploration of how American writers have depicted evil over the past three centuries, Andrew Delbanco reminds us that we—liberal and conservative alike— have always seen our nation as a "fortress of virtue." It is no coincidence that in the mid-1990s the groups singled out for relentless abuse and condemnation were welfare mothers and aliens, groups that were both powerless and, by virtue of color and nationality, capable of being depicted as threatening outsiders. Faced with undeniable evidence that we are neither virtuous nor isolated from the casual cruelties of our age, we seek again to focus our frustrations on the "blamable other," in Delbanco's phrase, "who can always be counted on to spare us the exigencies of examining ourselves."[92]

92. Andrew Delbanco, *The Death of Satan: How Americans Have Lost the Sense of Evil* (New York: Farrar, Straus & Giroux, 1995), 234.

INDEX